TRIPLE H:
MAKING The GAME

TRIPLE H: MAKING The GAME

Triple H

with Robert Caprio

POCKET BOOKS

New York   London   Toronto   Sydney

World Wrestling Entertainment® BOOKS

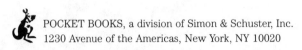

To my parents, for all their love and support throughout the years. I figure they deserve something after letting me eat them out of house and home. . . . And to every kid who has a dream and has the heart and soul to follow that dream.

Whenever I'm out in public, there are two questions people always ask me. How did I get to where I am in the wrestling business, and what tips can I give them on working out?

To some, the questions may seem unrelated, but for me, they cannot be separated. Becoming a serious

weight lifter as a teenager prepared me—both physically and mentally—to fulfill my dream of becoming a professional wrestler.

Weight training transformed me from a hundred-and-thirty-five-pound beanpole to someone who was entering bodybuilding competitions a few years later. It taught me how to set goals and remain focused on my quest to achieve them. It gave me self-confidence.

Many of the relationships that introduced me to the world of professional wrestling had their roots in the gym. And once I was in the wrestling business, my dedication to weight training and the lessons I learned through it helped me overcome challenges and continually shoot my career to the next level.

This book isn't an exact blueprint on how to turn yourself into a two-hundred-sixty-pound World Heavyweight Champion.

This is a workout book that will give you training tips, exercise examples, and information on nutrition and eating properly, all designed to put you on the road to an improved physique and a healthier lifestyle.

It's the story of how a kid from New Hampshire worked himself to the top of the professional wrestling industry.

Most importantly, this book explains how working out led to my professional success.

Whether you're trying to become the best player on your high school football team, live a healthier lifestyle, look good at the beach, or just want to give yourself a better shot with the babe down the block, I believe a dedication to weight training will provide the structure to help you achieve your goals.

It certainly did for me.

TRIPLE H: MAKING The GAME

Even though I was years away from stepping inside a ring, my wrestling career started on a summer day when I was fourteen years old. One of my buddies had just gotten his driver's license, and the two of us were out driving around when we passed a sign for a new

1. THE JOURNEY BEGINS

gym in town. They were giving away one-week passes to anyone who came in to check it out.

The first thing I saw when we walked in were these two jacked-up guys training on the bench press, and I thought, *Holy shit . . . this is awesome!* I'd had a weight bench at home and would mess around a bit on it—never anything serious, but enough to be aware of bodybuilding. One of the big things I'd always admired about bodybuilders—and wrestlers, for that matter— was their physiques. They were big, strong, powerful people who all seemed larger than life. The gym was busy that day, packed with all these guys who looked like the pictures I had seen.

They set us up with a program for our free week, and I never stopped going. It wasn't exactly a conscious decision I made, like, *I need to lift weights to look like these guys.* It was more that these were the coolest guys I'd ever seen and I was about to enter their world. It was the whole atmosphere that I wanted to be around.

I always had a paper route when I was a kid so I had money for myself. My parents told me that if joining the gym was something I wanted to do and had the money for, I should go ahead and do it. One of the great things about my parents was, they always supported everything I did. They were

Before wrestling and weight training entered my life, Little League baseball was one of my early pastimes.

the kind of parents who didn't only come to my Little League games, they worked in the concession stand too.

I'm sure the last thing my parents wanted to start doing was shuttle me back and forth to the gym every day, but they did. And they never complained to me about it.

The gym—Muscles In Motion—was where I started spending all of my free time. It became my home away from home. There were a couple of things about the atmosphere of the place that drew me in right way. The first was that it was what I consider a hard-core gym.

I remember that the way the place was decorated wouldn't have led you to use the word "hard-core" when describing it. The equipment was all done up with shiny chrome and yellow fabric, giving the impression that it was a froufrou gym, but it was just the opposite.

You ever been to a gym where there are twenty people in the exercise room, but not one of them is breaking a sweat? Everyone is standing around talking, laughing, having a good old time. Everyone's biggest concern is turning the gym into a meat market. That is not what my gym was.

You could walk in at six-thirty any night of the week and the weight room would be mobbed and the aerobics room packed. I mean, it was also a meat market—there were a lot of people trying to get laid in there—but for most of us, training was the primary focus.

There would be at least ten guys busting their balls in the weight room at any time. The attitude was serious. The people in there trained hard all the time. There was nobody sitting on the bench press machine for twenty minutes reading a newspaper and not performing a single exercise. That was the atmosphere I always wanted to be around.

And everybody knew everybody. Everybody supported everybody. It was like a family. If one guy from our gym was competing in a bodybuilding contest, the entire gym would be there to cheer him on. If one of the regulars was going for a personal best on his squat, every person in the gym would stop what they were doing to come over and encourage him. This attitude, this atmosphere, made it so easy for me to become a gym rat right away. I mean, as soon as I started training in this gym I was taking the lifestyle seriously, doing things like bringing a cooler to school every day that was loaded with bodybuilding staples like chicken breasts and pasta. I don't think my friends in school understood what I was doing or why, but that never bothered me. Once I got involved with the gym, I didn't spend much time with my high school classmates anyway. I didn't have much in common with anyone outside the tight-knit circle of people at the gym. I admired their drive to achieve their goals. They became my friends.

One of the first people at the gym to really bring me into their universe was Brian Zagorites. Brian personified why I was drawn to the gym. At twenty-one, he was the biggest guy in the place. And he just had a look to him. A look that made you know he was the coolest guy there. He had blond hair shaped in that flat-top Brian Bosworth style that was huge in the eighties and an intensity level that no one in the gym could match. If the gym was a fraternity, Brian would have been the president. He was a living example of what I wanted to get out of training.

A few months after I started at Muscles In Motion, I was talking to Brian one day as he worked the front desk and I waited for my workout partner. When it became clear that the guy I was supposed to train with that day wasn't going to show, Brian said that if I didn't mind sticking around a few hours for him to finish his shift, we could work out together. My immediate reaction was something like, *Hell, yeah, I'll wait!* For me, the chance to work out with Brian was like a combination of meeting the President and getting up onstage to perform with AC/DC.

The training session that followed was a gut-wrenching test of perseverance. Brian outweighed me by a hundred pounds and was making me do the same hard-core, high-volume sets as him. I was determined to hang with him. I matched him set for set, though I didn't even try to match him in weight. The next day, I couldn't even lift my arms past my shoulders without wincing in pain. It was a week before I could move my chest. He slaughtered me that night, but I didn't care. I was right back at the gym the next day, ready to train with him again and take the punishment. From that point on, I was "in" with the guys at the gym.

Looking back on it, I think I was like the gym mascot. I would work my way in with their sets—and I didn't care what they were training. Sometimes I'd be putting out so much effort that after a set I would go and puke, then come back in and ask, "Is it my turn again?" I refused to give up. Here was this fourteen-year-old, one-hundred-forty-pound kid, gangly, busting his ass with these bigger guys. When I first worked in with them, they were probably figuring they'd make me so sore I'd never show up again. But that didn't happen. I kept coming back every single night, and they respected that. They all looked at me and saw that although I was small, I was in there killing myself trying to hang with them. And that was all that mattered to them. That earned their respect. They didn't give a shit how old I was, how big I was, none of that. To them I was a bodybuilder just like them.

At first I think my mom was a bit concerned that here I was hanging out with all these huge guys from the gym who were in their twenties. There were days on the weekend where I'd have my mom drop me off at the gym, then I'd call her later and say, "Hey, Mom, the guys are all going out to grab some lunch, so I'm going to go with them, okay?" She would always let me go, but I know deep down she was curious about why the hell they were hanging out with me.

It just got back to that attitude, the family atmosphere that I loved so much about this gym. If it was a squat day, four or five of us would show up ready to spend the afternoon squatting. It was a club, something I wanted to be a part of, and these guys had no problem including me. Sometimes I think they forgot how old I was, though. There'd be nights where they'd want me to go with them out to the nightclubs. "We're heading over to The Bounty when we're done in here. They got a special dance contest going on tonight!" They lost sight of the fact that I was only fifteen, because in the gym we were all doing the same thing.

My parents wanted to come to the gym one day to meet all the guys I was hanging with now. After they saw how much these guys genuinely liked me and how important training was for me, they didn't have a problem with it. They realized that I wasn't out on the street, smoking or doing drugs. I was exercising. I was dedicating myself to something positive.

Training and spending quality time in the gym became my passion. After about three years of training with Brian and the rest of the guys down at Muscles In Motion, my physique had developed to the point where I was competing in regional bodybuilding contests—even winning Teen Mr. New Hampshire. I never seriously considered becoming a pro bodybuilder, though. It wasn't my dream. My dream was World Wrestling Federation.

By the time I was seventeen, I had developed into a six-foot-four, two-hundred-ten-pound high schooler who everyone wanted on the football and wrestling teams. But I wasn't into either of them. The last thing I wanted was to get run ragged and lose valuable size by going to football practice every afternoon or starving myself to make a specific weight for the wrestling tournaments.

It had already been such a long time since I participated in competitive sports that I just wasn't interested. I mean, I played Little League baseball and City League basketball when I was younger, but by the time I hit junior high, professional wrestling was the only athletic event I was concerned with. Although I didn't make a tin foil belt that I walked around with all the

One of my very first titles was Teen Mr. New Hampshire.

time, I was a dedicated fan. I subscribed to all the magazines and spent my entire Saturday watching wrestling on TV. Whenever a show came to the area, I would beg my dad to take me. The Boston Red Sox, Boston Celtics, and New England Patriots did nothing for me. Professional wrestling was the only game in town.

To this day, I don't care much about anything other than pro wrestling. It's not that I don't respect the athletes for being able to do what they do, I'm just not that interested in it. I can't hit a golf ball worth shit, so I'm amazed at what Tiger Woods can do out on that course. Ping-Pong players, tennis players, baseball players, every sport—I have all the respect in the world for those men and women as athletes. I just don't follow them.

I'll give you a good example. One night at a Pay-Per-View I was in the back going through final preparations for my match, which was coming up in a couple of minutes. There was some guy hanging out backstage. He obviously wasn't one of the boys, the other wrestlers, and I didn't recognize him as being someone from the office. He was standing around just sort of watching. Then he asked me a couple of times to autograph some photos. The first few times I didn't answer because I was going over plans for my match. After a while I couldn't take it anymore so I told him he had to get the hell out of the way. After he left, one of the other boys came over and told me that it was Dan Marino. I didn't even recognize one of the greatest quarterbacks in the history of the NFL. I have all the respect in the world for what Dan accomplished on the field, but I don't pay enough attention to the NFL to know what he actually looks like outside of a football helmet. I wanted to apologize to him after my match, but I wasn't really sure how to do that. I mean, if I went up to him and said I was sorry but I didn't recognize him or know who he was, would he have gotten offended? I didn't know how to approach it. As it turns out, he had left anyway, so I didn't have to worry about the actual apology.

So with high school football and amateur wrestling out of the question, I looked to the future. As a teenager with the size that I had, I started to think that maybe one day if I kept training hard I'd be able to give my dream of professional wrestling a try. I just never knew exactly how I'd break into it or find out where to start. There weren't a ton of wrestling schools at the time, and the ones that did exist weren't exactly advertised in the phone book. The business was so much different back then. People who were in it were protective of it, so you had to gain their trust before they would tell you how to get started. It was almost like a secret society. You had to know somebody on the inside before you got there.

My "in" came when I started working out with a power lifter named Ted Arcidi who had a brief career as a professional wrestler. Although he was reluctant at first, Ted was about to lead me to the next important stop on my rise to the top of World Wrestling Entertainment—Walter "Killer" Kowalski's Pro Wrestling School.

I am not Ron Simmons.

And neither are you.

Ron Simmons is a genetic freak.

I've never seen Ron in the gym. I don't think he even works out that much. If he never lifted a weight in his

2. GETTING DOWN TO BASICS

life, he would still look amazing. That's just how his body is. I'm not like that—I need to work my ass off to get results. So do most other people.

A lot of people think I only started lifting weights when I joined World Wrestling Federation, but I've been training seriously for over twenty years. I've done a lot with my physique during that time. In the first eight years of my training, I went from a hundred-thirty-five-pound gangly teenager to a two-hundred-seventy-five-pound solid young man getting his wrestling career on track. My guess is that you won't need to put on that much muscle mass, but regardless of your end goal, the first thing you have to do is physically walk into a gym. It's the way every single weight trainer's career starts. I did it one summer afternoon in Nashua, and now it's time for you to do it.

I know that a lot of people are intimidated by the gym. They think the muscular guys and the toned women, the regulars, are going to point and laugh. But I'm going to let you in on a secret—that's bullshit. Sure, you got your idiots at the gym just like you have anywhere you go, but you'll find that the majority of regulars at the gym are more interested in helping you than they are in picking on you. People who train on a regular basis, like me, believe in the importance of training so strongly that we welcome the chance to recruit some new people into our way of life. When I'm working out at the WWE Headquarters in Stamford, Connecticut, and see someone from the office in there busting their ass, but not really having a clue what they're doing, I wish they would ask me for some guidance. I'd love to help them out, but I don't want to stick my nose in without being asked.

As long as I see that person working hard, that's what's important. We all started somewhere. I think you'll find that most people at a gym feel this way. The only thing they care about is your effort. Whether you're five hundred pounds trying to drop weight or ninety-eight pounds trying to gain some, it doesn't matter. As long as you're working hard.

Now that you've built up the courage to get in the gym, let me give you five reasons why you should put in the time to train with consistency:

1. **Increased strength**

2. **Improved self-confidence**

3. **Injury prevention**

4. **Self-discipline**

5. **Sex (Trust me, you'll have a better shot with the ladies if you're in shape.)**

If you put in your time in the gym and don't cheat yourself when you're in there, these are only five of the things you'll accomplish. And some of these—improved self-confidence and self-discipline, for example—can lead you down a path to achieving more of your personal, grander goals in life.

One of the things that have confused me over the past few years is why weight training has become so complicated. The hard-core body-builders who I always tried to emulate—great champions like Arnold Schwarzenegger, Lee Haney, and Dorian Yates—stuck with free weight exercises and basic routines. The "meat-and-potatoes" of the gym.

You should start your training career with these basic mass-building exercises. Too many newcomers go in the gym, see a bunch of high-tech machines, and end up taking too many shortcuts without paying dues. Barbell and dumbbell exercises—free weight movements that will kick your ass every time out—are the best introduction to bodybuilding.

At the end of this chapter, I'm going to lay out a solid basic workout to introduce you to the world of bodybuilding. Don't look at this program and think, *Looks great, but this is just for beginners.* I hate the term "beginner" to describe a newcomer in the gym. A beginner makes you sound like a guy who is just goofing around, a novice in search of a clue. This is not some little workout that any jerk can do in his spare time.

Ronnie Coleman, a five-time Mr. Olympia, followed a split routine much like this one for many years. He adapted the reps, sets, and amounts of weight to help him meet his goals. And it worked just fine for him. However, if you truly believe that you're stagnating in the gym, that you've hit a plateau in your workouts and need to kick up the challenge, then you should move on to my more advanced workout routine that I lay out later in the book—but that shouldn't happen for a while.

This basic plan gets you set up for the road ahead. It will allow your body to adapt to progressive-resistance training, which is the key to making gains. The idea behind progressive-resistance training is to constantly increase your output so your body must adapt to the ever-increasing stress by getting bigger and stronger.

With this method, you're either adding more weight or completing more reps with each week. If on the barbell curls one week you do 8 reps at 50 pounds, try for 10 reps at that weight or throw an extra couple pounds on and work at getting 8 reps done again the following week. These increases may seem subtle, but they are affecting your body in a positive way. Your body is getting bigger, creeping toward your ultimate goal.

Think of your body as an engine. If you're a 10-horsepower engine and you add an 11-horsepower load, then you will convert and upgrade the engine to handle 11-horsepower loads. But if you try to put a 20-horsepower load on the engine, it will overheat and flame out, unable to adapt to that crushing load.

You have to take the process of building your body slow and steady. Take it a little bit at a time and you will make tremendous gains in the end.

The longer you stay on the basic program—even if it's years—the further ahead you'll be in the end. Forget about instant gratification. Amazing transformations, like the one that turned Peter Parker into Spider-Man, are not realistic—no matter how hard you go at it in the gym.

With this basic program, you want to train for a brief period of time as hard as you can. Whether you're doing high reps/lower weight or high weight/fewer reps, your intensity should never dip below your maximum level on each set.

Look to do between two and four sets per exercise. As for number of reps, you need to first choose the weight you'll work with on a set, then complete the maximum number of reps that you can at that weight with perfect form. This is referred to as working to failure. You're doing reps until you hit a point of momentary muscle failure and you can't squeeze out one more rep without compromising your form.

As you'll see when we lay out the schedule, the basic program is broken down into four days, split into two muscle groups. Meaning, you'll hit each muscle group twice each week. One day will be a "heavy day" where we'll look to put up more weight and get between 6 and 10 reps. The other will be a "light day" where the goal is 12 to 15 reps with a lighter weight load.

When you're just starting out, I recommend a four-day split that combines chest, shoulders, and triceps on days one and three, and then working your back, biceps, and legs on days two and four.

The goal is to select two exercises per body part and stick with the basics.

DAYS ONE & THREE

Flat- and incline-bench presses yield big results for your pecs.

Chest

Do pressing movements that will build the size and strength of the pectoral muscles of the chest. Exercises like flat- and incline-bench presses, with either a barbell or dumbbells, are the best mass-building movements at the outset. Once you gain complete confidence with these staples of size and strength, feel free to move on to flys—both flat and incline variations.

Shoulders

Dumbbell presses to build the entire shoulder capsule and upright rows for added quality from front to back. Lateral raises—also referred to as side laterals—hit the medial (side) deltoid, which adds width and V-taper and helps to make the waist look smaller.

Dumbbell presses work my entire shoulders and help me achieve a V-shaped form.

The rope-handle pressdown is an easy exercise that works the triceps hard.

Triceps

Triceps pressdowns, with either a V-bar or a rope handle, bring out the horse-shoe shape of the muscle. It's a controlled, easy-to-master exercise that will lay the foundation for more advanced exercises such as French presses and lying triceps extensions with an E-Z Curl bar.

Back

Wide-grip pulldowns, either to the front or to the back, to develop the width of the upper lats, and dumbbell rows for upper and lower lats. Wait on the deadlifts and barbell rows until you have built up your base of strength. Once the foundation is set, you can tweak the program and modify as needed.

Biceps

Dumbbell and barbell curls both work the overall biceps muscles. Barbell curls also target forearm flexors. Dumbbell curls force each arm to independently handle the load, which prevents the weaker arm from slacking out of getting its fair share of resistance. Unilateral (one arm at a time) training helps to improve symmetry by making sure that each side of the body balances out for strength and size.

TRIPLE H

Legs

Leg extensions will define and shape the front of the quadriceps (thigh) muscles. Leg presses pack size onto the quads without the wear and tear that squats put on the lower back and knees. If your body can handle the stress, though, squats are still the best exercise. Leg curls are the best hamstring exercise, while calf raises will prod the hard-to-train calves into growth mode.

MARK IT DOWN: KEEP A TRAINING LOG

Before you go and actually hit the weights, there are two things you must have—a gym to go work out in and a notebook or journal to keep track of what you're doing there.

Forget about building a better body if you don't know what you've accomplished or when it's time to move up to the next level of training. Sure, you might be able to tell just by looking in the mirror that training is working

Two of the most important items in my gym are the pen and paper I use to keep a daily record of my progress.

or it's time to step it up, but the only way to be certain that you're ready to make a change is to keep meticulous records of your progress.

A training diary allows you to look back at what you've accomplished over the past few months and prove that your strength has progressed. That all this work you're putting in at the gym is getting you somewhere. Being able to go through a journal and see that you're lifting considerably more weight than you were six months ago is a great way to keep motivated. And if you look back and see that in the past few weeks you've sort of hit a plateau, you haven't increased weight in a while, well then, it's time to step up the intensity of your workouts.

In addition to keeping written records of your workouts, it's also good to chart everything you're eating. Your diet and your progress in the gym are connected. There's no argument about that. Keeping track of what you're eating and how it's affecting your workouts—learning what's stimulating progress and what's hindering it—is the only way you can see the big picture and make sure you're giving your body what it needs to get closer to your goals.

If you go through a period where you're ripping it up at the gym every time in, you need to go back and see what you were eating at the time to make sure you keep on that path. If you're feeling sluggish for a week or two, go back and look at what you've been taking in. Did you change anything? Did you up your intake of carbs? Lower your protein? The only way to take the guesswork out of it and know what's really going on is to keep a training log.

Later on in the book, I'm going to tell you how I destroyed my left leg during a match and worked my ass off to come back from it. Rehabbing that leg was the hardest thing I ever had to do. One of the main reasons I was able to get through those long, strenuous days of rehab was that I kept a detailed training log.

I knew that the keys—besides physical therapy—were to jack up my protein intake and increase my calories while remaining wary of getting too fat. My training and nutrition diary allowed me to see that I could handle a lot more protein and calories in my diet without putting on any significant body fat. I learned that the increased protein led to increased productivity in the gym. I could see the connection between the changes I was making in my diet and the progress I was making in rehab. This documented proof of progress kept me optimistic during a challenging time.

Your training log doesn't have to be some elaborate chart. Keep it simple. For every meal you eat during the day—and this includes protein shakes and other meal replacements—describe everything you ate, record what time you ate it, how many total grams of protein, carbohydrates, fat, and calories you took in. Then make a note of how you felt at the end of the day. Were you energized, dehydrated, sluggish?

The same thing goes for your workouts. Record the date and exact time you went to the gym and when you left. Write down every exercise performed. How many sets, reps, and what weight you were putting up for each. Make sure to comment on how you felt before you walked into the gym, in the middle of your workout, and when you left.

This might seem like homework to some of you right now. But trust me, in six months you'll be stoked to be able to look back and see in your own handwriting how far you've come along.

TRAINING SCHEDULE

Start the week with heavier weights and then alternate to a more endurance-oriented session the second day in. The lighter workout is no less intense—even though you are lifting with lower poundages. There's nothing *easy* about high-rep workouts if you stay after the pump with a one-hundred-percent effort and all-out focus.

If it's possible, your workout days should be Monday, Tuesday, Thursday, and Friday. With the four-day splits, this rotation will give your body two full days off between each cycle.

THE BASIC BODYBUILDING WORKOUT

Day One (HEAVY DAY)

CHEST, SHOULDERS, TRICEPS

EXERCISE	SETS	REPS
Incline-bench presses	2–4	6–10
Flat-bench presses	2–4	6–10
Dumbbell presses	2–4	6–10
Lateral raises or upright rows	2–4	6–10
Triceps pushdowns	2–4	6–10
Lying triceps extensions	2–4	6–10

TRIPLE H

Day Two (LIGHT DAY)

BACK, BICEPS, LEGS

EXERCISE	SETS	REPS
Wide-grip pulldowns	2–4	12–15
Dumbbell rows	2–4	12–15
Hyperextensions	1–2	10–15
Dumbbell curls	2–4	12–15
Barbell curls	2–4	12–15
Leg extensions	2–4	12–15
Leg presses	2–4	12–15
Leg curls	2–4	6–10
Calf raises	2–4	6–10

Day Three (LIGHT DAY)

CHEST, SHOULDERS, TRICEPS

EXERCISE	SETS	REPS
Incline-bench presses	2–4	12–15
Flat-bench presses	2–4	12–15
Dumbbell presses	2–4	12–15
Lateral raises or upright rows	2–4	12–15
Triceps pushdowns	2–4	12–15
Lying triceps extensions	2–4	12–15

Day Four (HEAVY DAY)

BACK, BICEPS, LEGS

EXERCISE	SETS	REPS
Wide-grip pulldowns	2–4	6–10
Dumbbell rows	2–4	6–10
Hyperextensions	1–2	10–15
Dumbbell curls	2–4	6–10
Barbell curls	2–4	6–10
Leg extensions	2–4	6–10
Leg presses	2–4	6–10
Leg curls	2–4	6–10
Calf raises	2–4	6–10

I already knew who Ted Arcidi was when I met him. He had a brief pro wrestling career, pulling stints in both World Wrestling Federation and World Class Wrestling down in Texas with the Von Erichs. He was also a decorated power lifter as he was the first person to bench-

press over 700 pounds when he put up 705 in 1985. This was a major accomplishment in the power lifting world and a record that stood for a while.

Now even though he was able to make some money as a wrestler, whenever I'd talk to Ted about the business, he'd try his best to steer me away from it. Ted never wanted to be a wrestler; power lifting led him toward it and he only saw it as a way to make some quick money. Professional wrestling was never his dream. Because he hated the travel and never had the passion for the business that I did, he had a negative view of it when I met him.

When I'd ask him for some help on getting started, his answer was always the same. "It's a tough business," he'd tell me. "It's a tough business to break into, it's a tough business to make money in, and it's a tough business to have a future in. You don't want to get involved."

I think he saw me as this nice clean-cut kid who helped him out in the gym and had an interest in wrestling. I don't know if he saw what I was willing to give in order to succeed. That I'd be mentally strong enough to deal with all the bullshit to get to where I wanted. He thought I'd get eaten up in the wrestling business.

The truth is that if I had met myself at that age and worked in the business during the time when Ted did, I would've given the same kind of advice. I would've said, "Listen, kid, if you want to get into this business, you really gotta want it because it's not easy."

And I really wanted it. Since I wouldn't give up on my dream and kept asking him about it, Ted finally broke down and gave me the names of two wrestling schools in New England: Walter "Killer" Kowalski's school in Malden, Massachusetts, and a school in Orange, Connecticut, run by an old-time wrestler named Tony Altimore.

By this time, Muscles In Motion had closed down, which was a tough thing to deal with. We were all standing around on that last day when they were taking the equipment out and it was like watching a wrecking ball go through your mom's house where you grew up. So many memories, so many good times, all gone just like that. With our gym no longer there, we all moved over to the Gold's Gym in town. It didn't take us too long to get used to the Gold's—it was all the same people training, just in a different spot now. I even became the manager over at Gold's.

Now that I had the information from Ted I needed, I was ready to start my wrestling training. I was able to get in touch with Tony's gym right away.

Since I was not into the idea of moving to Connecticut, I cooked up a plan where I'd drive down there on weekends to learn how to wrestle and work my regular job at the Gold's Gym in Nashua during the week. Walter's gym—only one hour away from my home in New Hampshire—was a much better option, though. The only problem was, I couldn't get in touch with him. The numbers I'd gotten from Ted were old and no longer in service.

After running into a lot of dead ends searching for the working phone number, I lucked into it through a friend of a friend. Finally, I was able to talk to the legendary Walter "Killer" Kowalski.

Like Ted, Walter also came across as cynical about the business at first. He made sure you understood that the prospects of making a living as a wrestler weren't good. You have to understand that Walter's generation was protective about the business and this was one of his ways of making

The legendary Walter "Killer" Kowalski and me, "stylin' and profilin' " in a Ric Flair haircut.

sure you really wanted to be a part of it. Right away, he'd tell you how hard it is to survive. But if you were still willing to try it out at the end of that phone call, Walter was willing to let you come in and pay your money.

There was nothing fancy about Walter's school—and this was by design. It was another way he tested you, to establish that you really wanted to be in the business. We didn't learn in a wrestling ring, we learned in a boxing ring with no—and I mean no—give to it. It was slightly more forgiving than concrete. I watched so many kids get slammed down on that thing for the first time and get this look in their eye like, *What the hell am I doing here? I can't do this shit.*

When I introduced myself to Walter, the first thing out of his mouth was, "You're a big one, ain't ya?" I could tell by the way he was sizing me up that he saw something he liked in me. He was used to working with a bunch of skinny kids trying to be wrestlers and here I was this six-foot-four, two-hundred-sixty-pound guy ready to go. I know in his mind he was thinking, *I could really do something with this kid here.*

A few minutes after I arrived, I was introduced to another one of Walter's tests. A drill he called "The Hard Way In." Basically, he made every guy stand just on the outside of the ring, hold on to the top rope, then flip themselves up and over it to land inside the ring, flat on their backs.

Walter came across like the least sympathetic teacher on the face of the earth. These poor guys were killing themselves, landing on their heads so hard they could barely get up off the mat, and he was screaming at them the whole time. "You guys are shit! You're pathetic! Get out of my school!"

He was very harsh, but I know he was trying to toughen them up.

Walter looked over at me and told me to do the move. I explained that I'd never even been in a ring before, but he didn't care. As I took hold of the top rope, I figured I was about to kill myself. I was wrong. I nailed it dead-on.

Walter killed all the other guys. Yelling at them about how easy this move was, how I was an absolute beginner and got it right the first time I ever set foot near a ring.

When I got back home that night, my girlfriend at the time asked me how it went and I told her, "You know, it was the most comfortable I ever felt doing something the first time in my life. I felt at home."

Even though I was beat up, sore as shit, and black and blue, I couldn't wait to get back. It was the dead of summer so the place was a thousand degrees and I was getting slammed into a solid steel ring, but I didn't care about any of that. It felt right on the inside. From that very first day it felt like something I was supposed to do.

Walter put a lot of energy into my career. He assured me that I had the look, size, and charisma to be a star. I started training at the school four nights a week and spent the rest of my time managing the Gold's Gym back in Nashua.

The fact that Walter believed in me, that he jumped in the ring with me every time I got in there to give me all this advice that he wasn't giving to the other guys, gave me a ton of confidence in my ability to make it. At the same time, though, I've always been a realistic person. I remember thinking, *You know, I'm gonna give this a try. I'm gonna give this a few years and if I don't feel like I'm on the right path to the top . . . I'm out.*

There were so many guys at the school who let you know that their big goal was to just get on Saturday morning TV to be one of the guys who gets

My idea of working in a mall was
far different from most people's.

squashed. And I'd be thinking, *Why the hell would you want to do that? I want to be the guy doing the squashing!* These other guys all just wanted to be able to say they were wrestlers. Not me. I wanted to be in the big time. I wanted to be Ric Flair. I wanted to be the best. And if I didn't see myself getting there, I was going to move on to something else.

No matter what you go after in life, if you're gonna do it, do it all the way, but at the same time, prepare yourself for the reality.

In those days of training at Walter's, I'd go to the school and keep up with my responsibilities back at Gold's. I was still doing everything I was doing before I started working to become a wrestler. Even though I started working independents on the weekend, I kept working at my day job.

In fact, I never stopped working at Gold's until I got hired by WCW—World Championship Wrestling. I think that showing this level of responsibility went a long way toward gaining my parents' support—especially my mother's. When I first told her that I was going to wrestling school, she was concerned that it wasn't a "stable job." By my never giving up my day job the entire time I was working the independent scene in the Northeast, she saw that I wasn't just dropping everything I had to follow some dream that may or may not work out. My dad was a bit more behind me and did a lot to convince my mom that this was something they should support. One of his better lines about it was, "Let him get it out of his system. Remember, I went to school for a couple of things that I never ended up becoming, so what's the difference here?" Knowing I had their full support while I pursued my dream meant so much to me.

In addition to his wrestling school, Walter had his own independent outfit, the IWF, the International Wrestling Federation. The IWF was like most independent organizations—which meant a lot of wacky shit went on.

One of the best stories from this time is the one that ended up giving me the name I'd wrestle under for the next few years. About three months after I started at Walter's, he came up to me out of the blue and asked in that thick Polish accent of his, "Do you have a valid passport?"

Seeing as I'd pretty much never been out of the Northeast, I let him know I didn't. He went on, looking me straight in the eye, as serious as could be. "Okay then, you need to go into Boston to get one today. You must go to one of those places that are open twenty-four hours and give you a passport immediately. We are leaving for a wrestling tour of South America very soon."

I couldn't believe it. Here I was, a wrestling student for only three months, and I was already going on an international tour. As you could imagine, I was stoked. I told Walter I'd get the passport and whatever else I needed for the trip. And there *was* one other thing he needed from me.

"We also need to figure out a name for you today," he said. "I am going to get posters printed up to advertise down there and I want you on them." His first suggestion was that I carry on the legacy of a guy who'd just left the IWF—Jake Scream. His whole gimmick was that he'd scream the entire match. He'd wrestle like everyone else, but scream while he was doing it. Walter liked the gimmick so much that he wanted me to take on a different first name and work as Jake Scream's cousin to carry on the tradition.

"You know, Walter, I just don't know that I'd feel comfortable screaming the whole time I'm in the ring."

"Okay then, we'll call you . . . The Terrorizer!"

"The Terrorizer? That seems kind of hokey. Like you might as well call me

The Crusher or something," I said. To Walter's defense, this was the era he wrestled in, where these were the kind of names everyone had.

"Oh, you don't like that either? Well, God damn it then, you pick something."

Now I was thinking that I'd pissed him off and you sure as hell never wanted to piss him off. So I tried to smooth the whole thing over. "It's not that bad, Walter, I was just thinking I'd have more of a real name. You know what I mean? Not like The Bruiser or The Crusher."

"Well, okay then. I have to tell the guy tomorrow so I'll figure it out."

What he figured out was to go back to The Terrorizer, take off "The" and split Terrorizer down the middle to end up with the name Terror Riser. Even though the tour to South America never happened—it was just another one of Walter's crazy schemes that never came through—he was dead-set on me keeping the name, so I had to deal with it.

I tried to adapt it and turn it into a name that might seem more real. At the time, Andre Rison was a big NFL star so I thought it would be possible to pull it off if I messed around with the spelling a bit. I thought to spell the first name Terra, because I figured that was more likely to be someone's name than Terror. And for the last name I went with Ryzing. I became Terra Ryzing, which I thought was the best I could do with it. If I had known that later on in my career I would continue to work under the name Terra Ryzing thanks to the disorganization of the WCW office, I might not have been so willing to take it on for Walter. But what the hell did I know?

With the South American trip canceled, I made my debut a few weeks later in Burlington, Vermont. You know, I watched the tape of it again a few years ago, and I wasn't as bad as I would have thought I'd been. For my first

match, it wasn't horrendous. I see guys starting out now and I'm like, *Oh shit, he is not good. He is not going to make it.* I mean, I did all the clichéd wrestling moves and all that, but it wasn't horrible.

Thinking back to the actual day, I don't remember too many details about the match, but there is one thing that sticks out in my mind about the event. Like most of the places you work when you're on the independent scene, the locker room that night was small. Nothing fancy—just an open space with a couple of benches and a place to store and hang your stuff. Over in the corner, though, there was a little office that had a plaque hanging outside of it that read: The Vincent K. McMahon Office. I remember looking at that thing and thinking, *Holy shit! When World Wrestling Federation comes here, this is where Vince actually sits. He's been in this room!* He got such a kick out of that story when I told him years later.

Long before I was The Game, the IWF knew me as "Terra Ryzing."

I also got my official introduction into professional wrestling that night by receiving only half of the fifty dollars I was promised. I got ripped off in my debut, which is the way it should be, so you learn right away that you can't trust everybody's word in this business.

My wrestling was progressing at a quick rate. About six months after I'd started, Walter came over to me one day and said, "Next Saturday, I'm going to put the title on you. You are the top guy."

For the next few months I was having a blast touring around northern New England and eastern Canada with the IWF title. I was getting my ass kicked and not making any money—I was actually losing money, with all my expenses—but I was having too much fun to worry about it.

After a couple of months of this, I felt like I was getting better and started to think seriously about leaving Walter's to move on to something bigger. I believed I was the best guy at Walter's, but that's not saying much. It was kind of like being the fastest kid in your neighborhood. Big deal. So I started to wonder about my future.

Then one night, Pat Patterson, the top WWE agent and talent scout at the time, showed up at our event to see if there was anyone who had the goods to make it to the big time.

He talked to me after the show to let me know he liked what he saw. He encouraged me to stick with it because he could see my potential. This was big. To a young wrestler looking for his big break, after Vince, Pat was the most important person in the entire industry to know. So for him to have some positive words for me was a huge deal.

On the other hand, though, I about shit myself because I started thinking, *What if they call me tomorrow to say they want to take a look*

Holding the IWF title
wasn't profitable, but
it sure was fun.

at me? I wasn't ready. I was improving, but I knew I wasn't good enough just yet.

Now I *knew* I had to take a step up from Walter's. I had to go somewhere. Just not there, not yet.

Determined to make a move soon, I put some time and money into marketing myself to larger promotions. I got some new pictures done, put together a tape of some of my matches, and threw together a bogus resume. I wrote that I'd been wrestling for like five years, when I'd really only been doing it for one. I just made up stuff. Completely bullshitted. And I put it all together in a little package like I was trying to get a regular job. I figured that if I had a regular job, like a stockbroker, and was looking to move to a new firm, this is what I would do, so why not do it to get a new job in the professional wrestling industry?

When I finished the package, I sent it out to different people. I sent one to Memphis, and they were interested in me. I had an offer from Japan that just wasn't for enough money to survive on. It would have been a great experience, but I would have come back losing way too much money.

The Memphis thing interested me because I felt like it was a realistic next step. Although I knew it would offer very little cash, I'd be able to get experience with TV.

One of the big problems with Memphis was that I knew that nobody was making any money down there. Some of the other guys I trained with had gone, and no one was making shit. I figured the only way I could do it was if I got a second job bouncing or working at a gym and went down there with someone else to split expenses. Only having to worry about paying half a rent would take off a lot of the burden.

The first person I thought of was this guy Tony who also went to Walter's. Tony started his training three or four years before I did, so he'd been at it awhile now and was still doing just local stuff around the school. I figured he'd be ready to step it up a bit, see if he could really make it.

So I go to his house one day to tell him that I was heading down to Memphis and thought he should come with me. "Ehhh, I don't know. I'm not real great with leaving home, you know?" Now, this guy didn't have an actual job. All he did was wrestle occasionally on the weekends. It's not like he didn't have the time to work on the side, he just didn't want to. Instead, he just lived at home and sponged off his parents.

I didn't really have any other options, so I wouldn't let him off easy. "Tony, how in the hell do you plan on being a professional wrestler if you won't leave home? Can I ask you that? Have you actually thought about this? They travel all around the world. What are you going to do, bring your folks with you?" He didn't have an answer; he just kind of shrugged his shoulders. I remember being so baffled with this that I just got up and walked out of there.

A few years ago, I was visiting my parents back at home and stopped off at the supplement store one afternoon. And right there posted on the wall was a flyer with this guy's wrestling picture on it! I couldn't help but laugh seeing that he was still at it. The woman behind the counter asked me if I knew Tony.

"Yeah, we used to train together at the school back in the day. How's he doing?"

"Oh, you know, he's real good," she said. "Still wrestling. Still trying to make it."

Still trying to make it? Come on! He had to be thirty years old at the time and he was still plugging away at the regional stuff. To quote Pat Patterson, "Puhleeeeeze!" He did at least have a title belt on in the picture, which I'm sure made him feel better about the whole thing.

Thanks in part to Tony, the Memphis thing wasn't going to happen as fast as I would have liked. So I was still working hard—training at Walter's, managing the Gold's Gym—trying to figure out my next move, when a strange coincidence was brought to my attention. The consulting firm that we used for our sales department at the gym was the same one that Flair used for the Gold's that he owned.

The consulting people came up to our gym on a regular basis, and I got along real well with the guy who ran the company. After one of our meetings, he invited me out to their next seminar. I wasn't jumping at the chance to go, but he was able to quickly convince me. "Ric Flair is going to be there as a guest speaker." He knew I was a wrestler and thought I would be into seeing Flair. He was right.

I was sure that I wasn't going to meet Ric or anything like that, but I threw my resume in my bag just in case. As it turned out, I did get to meet him while I was there. We had a quick, polite conversation. Ric was nice enough, but typical Ric, he was more geared up to go out and have some fun, not hang around a marketing conference all night.

There was another guy from WCW who I met at the seminar and ended up hanging out with that night, though. Chip Burnham, a promoter and regional ticket salesman for WCW, stopped by the conference because he was thinking about investing in some gyms. That night a bunch of us went out and Jim started talking to me about the business because the other people we were with told him I was a wrestler. I could tell right after meeting him that Chip was a good guy. He was real easy to get along with, and right from the start we hit it off. As we were all taking off for the night, he said to me, "You should send me your resume and tape. I'm good friends with Bob Due, the president of WCW, so I'll make sure your info gets in the right hands. I don't know how you are in the ring, but I can tell you have the right attitude and a good head on your shoulders. You never know. Maybe they'll give you a call."

"Thanks, I appreciate that. But I don't need to send it to you . . . I've got everything right here." I reached into my bag and pulled out my resume package for him.

A few weeks later, I'm working at the gym when the front desk pages me. "You have a phone call from a man named Bob Due. Says he's with World Championship Wrestling." Now I don't know what to think. This is the president of WCW. Part of me was excited; part of me thought there was some kind of mistake. I finally pick up the line and sure as shit, it was Bob Due on the other end.

"Yeah, Jim gave me your stuff . . . yeah . . . it looks pretty impressive," he said. "I'm going to give it to Eric Bischoff, who's taking over the reins of the company. He's in Japan right now, so when he gets back he'll give you a call."

I'm obviously feeling real good after my call from Bob, but I didn't have any time to let my mind go because the same day I got a call from Bischoff. The very first thing he said to me on the phone wasn't hello, wasn't an introduction, it was, "How do you know Bob Due?" What he was really saying to me was, *Who the hell are you and why did I have the president of the*

company put your resume on my desk the first day I'm in the office with a note telling me to call you?

After I explained to Eric how Bob came across my resume, I was about to get into a discussion with the new head of WCW that, quite frankly, I don't know how I had the balls to do in my position.

One of the training mistakes I made early on was trying to do too many sets per body part. Back when I started out in the eighties, the "High Volume" method of training was the big thing. This basically meant a ton of sets. A high-volume trainer would go into the gym and do 25

sets of chest. He'd take five exercises and do 5 sets each exercise. I wish I knew then what I know now, because there's no way I would have put myself through all of that shit. In those days, a three-hour workout session was routine, and that is just totally unnecessary. I eventually learned this on my own, but I wouldn't have minded someone clueing me in when I first started out. So let me give you a couple of tips that may save you some grief along the way.

GIVE THAT MUSCLE A BREAK: DO NOT OVERTRAIN

I believe the best way to train is to stimulate your muscle—not kill it—just stimulate it, get a good pump running through it, then leave it alone and let it grow. When I started out with those marathon sessions that were taking up so much time, I was overtraining because I wasn't letting my muscles rest at all. It was all more, more, more.

Recovery is one of the least understood aspects of strength training. The great thing is that your body actually grows when you rest. That's one of the major reasons why anyone just starting out in the gym should only look to train three or four days a week. Your muscles will need to get used to the stimulation.

TRAIN WITH YOUR GOALS IN MIND

Someone who truly helped me understand how overtraining was counter-productive to my goals as a professional wrestler was Charles Glass, one of the most respected trainers in the world. He's the top personal trainer at what many refer to as "The Mecca of Bodybuilding"—Gold's Gym in Venice Beach, California. I met Charles while training out there one day in 1995. I was performing a typical shoulder workout when he came over to me and asked why I was doing a rear-delt fly without isolating the target muscle. He told me I needed to stick my butt back, turn my hands up, and pull more with my rear deltoid instead of using all three heads of the shoulder complex. I followed his advice for the rest of that workout, and I could immediately feel it making a difference.

I thanked Charles when I saw him the next day, and he couldn't have been nicer, praising my work ethic, then inviting me to train with him whenever I was in Los Angeles. I took him up on that offer, and then some. As you'll find out, I've relied on Charles for training tips a lot since that day. He has helped put a lot into perspective for me on training and nutrition.

One of the things he's pointed out to me over the years was that I was trying to do a strict bodybuilding workout that was too extreme given the punishment I take all the time in the ring. I'm on the road two hundred days a year, putting my body through hell every night. I can't also be tearing it up in the gym with too many exercises, too many sets, and too many reps. "You can't do the same workout that Lee Haney used to do!" is what I'd hear from Charles all the time. Lee was an eight-time Mr. Olympia who could absolutely punish his body in the gym because all he had to do when he was done training was rest—he didn't have to go wrestle.

Another one of Charles's favorite sayings was, "You have to scale back on the workouts to do what's right for you as a professional wrestler."

And you have to scale your workouts to do what's right for your personal goals.

THE MIND-MUSCLE CONNECTION

Weight training doesn't require only physical exertion. There's a mental aspect to it as well, what's sometimes referred to as the "mind-muscle connection." It's not an easy thing to describe, but let me give it a shot.

Think of it like this—when you're in the gym doing flat-bench dumbbell flys, don't just jump on the bench and start moving weights around while

30 IRON GRIP Seahawks

If you think weight training is all about building muscle, then your head's in the wrong place.

your mind wanders. Lie down on the bench and think about what you're doing with every rep. See the weights rise from your sides, up over your head, and visualize what is going on with your body. Focus on contracting your pecs every time those dumbbells make their way up. Feel the blood pumping into your target muscles.

It's another way to increase your intensity while you're training. I can assure you that the person who dedicates as much mental energy to his training as physical energy is going to make a whole hell of a lot faster progress than the person who completes sets between reading magazine articles for ten minutes a clip.

THIS IS A TWO-WAY STREET

This isn't so much a tip as it is just something to remember. It's one of the things about bodybuilding that I love. You get back from it exactly what you put into it. If you join a fancy gym that has all the latest technological innovations, but you half-ass every workout, you're not going to see any results. There's nothing complicated about training. You work hard at it, you'll get the results you want.

During a tour of Africa, I once trained inside a dilapidated wooden shack that sat in the middle of a grassy field. The shack had a few dumbbells. It had a weight bench and a funky lat pulldown machine made from a car seat, a pulley, and a rope attached to a pan with cinderblocks that lifted the weights up and down. Even with this equipment, I still had a killer workout. You can do the same type of thing with a home gym that has dumbbells, a weight bench, and a free bar.

You don't need all that special, high-end equipment to start training. You only need the desire to get it done.

If you're new to weight training, the program set out in Chapter 2 should keep you busy for some time. After a while, though, you may feel like you need to change your routine a bit, try some new things to keep it fresh. If you're getting bored working the same exercises week after week, there's a chance that one day you'll stop going to the gym. And that's exactly what we need to avoid.

Here are a few twists that you may want to add to your typical workout once in a while after you've gained some experience with the weights. By no means are these methods necessary, nor should they become a regular part of your workout, but they're things you could try if you're in the mood for something new.

Forced Repetitions

All training techniques increase your intensity. If you do 10 reps to failure, the way to increase the intensity is to force another one. Of course, if your body has stopped, you won't be able to pump out another rep, so you'll need to have someone help you—a spotter you trust.

This forced repetition increases your intensity. It pushes your muscle beyond its limit.

Forced reps are a way of adding a little bit of intensity without burning out your engine. But you need to be careful with forced reps. If you did 5 with every set you worked, you wouldn't last too long.

Rest-Pause Technique

I'm always looking for new ideas that will enable me to improve the effectiveness of my workouts. Recently, I picked up a great one from a video produced by Jay Cutler, an amazing bodybuilder and all-around intelligent guy.

Because I usually train on my own, I can't do forced reps all that often. Jay's video provided me a viable alternative called the rest-pause technique.

Let's say I'm doing preacher curls. I'll pump out as many reps as I can until I hit the point of failure. I'll put the weight down and rest for five or six seconds, then pick up the bar and hammer out two more reps that would have been impossible without the rest-pause technique.

I'd still prefer to do a forced rep with a partner helping me crank out that extra one or two past failure, but rest-pause is a great alternative when I'm training on my own.

The Triple H Burn

This is a tip that Charles Glass provided me during my rehab stint. It's a workout just for the legs. When my rehab progressed to where I was working with weights, I asked Charles to find a way to increase the intensity of leg training without the stress of too much weight.

The drop set that he introduced me to—what my physical therapist dubbed "The Triple H Burn"—helped rebuild the strength of my quads.

With no rest between sets, select a moderate weight and:

- **Do 15 reps on a leg press and hold the 15th rep for a count of 15 in the flexed position**

- **Do 12 reps, hold the 12th rep for a count of 12 in the flexed position**

- **Do 10 reps, hold the 10th rep for a count of 10 in the flexed position**

- **Do 7 reps, hold for a count of 7**

- **Do 6 reps, hold for a count of 6**

- **Do 5 reps, hold for a count of 5**

- **Do 4 reps, hold for a count of 4**

- **Do 3 reps, hold for a count of 3**

- **Do 2 reps, hold for a count of 2**

- **Do 1 rep, hold for a count of 1**

This workout is absolutely brutal. By the time you get through it your quads are on fire. Obviously, you can't do it every time you train, but throwing it in there every couple of workouts is a great way to shock the muscles, and it's safer and, I believe, more effective than just doing a few regular sets.

Forcing an extra rep now and then is a great way to keep your workout interesting.

Running the Rack

If you've spent any time around a gym, I'm sure you've heard this phrase thrown around at some point. When somebody "runs the rack" with an exercise, they're moving from one set right into the next, working to failure every time, decreasing the weight with each set. Someone running the rack on preacher curls may work 80 pounds to failure, then move right to 60 pounds and go to failure again. Then they may drop to 40, and then 20 before they finish up. You just need to decide how many sets you want to do before you start out so you know exactly what your weight decreases will be.

All of these variations are advanced methods of training. You should only consider trying any of them once you have an expert grasp of basic training. This should take you a few years.

"I just don't know," Bischoff said after we got through the explanation of how I got my resume into Bob Due's hands. "You don't have a name, I've never seen you work, and you're a G.U.D."

"I'm a what?"

"A G.U.D. It means you are Geographically UnDesirable."

To this day, I am convinced that Eric made up the term G.U.D. as a way to blow people off when he didn't want to hire them. I have still never heard anyone else in the business use this term.

"What does that mean?"

"It means that you are from New Hampshire, while we are based in Atlanta."

"Okay. So what does that have to do with anything?"

"It means that you live in New Hampshire, which is in the Northeast, and we are in Atlanta, which is far away in the South."

"Are you telling me that you're only hiring wrestlers who live in Atlanta?" I asked, genuinely confused at where he was going with all this.

"No, of course not."

"Well then, what difference does it make where I live now? I'd move to Atlanta if you want me to."

"Nah. I've never even seen you wrestle. I can't justify spending all that money to bring you down here when I've never even seen you work. What if you're rotten? Then I would have wasted all this money on the company's behalf to try out a rotten wrestler."

Now that I know of all the millions of dollars he was going to waste later on in his time at WCW, this conversation is quite funny to think about. At the time, though, I wasn't going to argue with him about money. I just wanted an opportunity.

"How about this . . . if you can promise me five minutes of your time to watch me wrestle, I'll pay my own way to Atlanta. I will fly myself down there and get a hotel. All you have to do is look at me."

He hemmed and hawed for a couple of minutes. "I don't know. I just . . . well . . . I don't know."

"I understand your reservation about paying for me, Mister Bischoff, but I can't understand your hesitation on this offer. You have absolutely no risk here." Part of me still can't believe I talked to him this way. He was the new head of WCW and I was a small-time wrestler looking for my big break in the business.

After a long silence, he spoke up. "You know, you got a point there. We have TV in two weeks. Someone from our travel department will be in touch with you in the next few days with all the details. See you there."

When I arrived in Atlanta, I immediately went to the Center Stage Theatre, where the tapings were held. Because it was so early, every door was locked. I walked around the building for a bit, then finally knocked on one toward the back. Dusty Rhodes, the American Dream, one of the biggest legends in the history of the business, opened the door. I was in awe!

"What you want, kid?" Dusty asked.

"Hello. My name is Paul Levesque. I'm here because I have a match tonight."

"Who said you have a match?"

"Eric Bischoff." As I said that name, I could see the expression on his face change. And not in a good way.

"Well, that's not your fault, I guess. Come on in."

What I didn't know was that Dusty was technically running things at the time and they were bringing in Eric to take over, but nobody had told Dusty yet. I found out later that this turned out to be a major fiasco that day. Dusty went right upstairs and started ripping people new ones, screaming at everyone who was there. "What's going on here? This Bischoff is bringing in new people for tryouts? The sonofabitch doesn't even work here!" Stuff like that, to try and figure out why some new kid had showed up at Bischoff's request.

I remember someone from the office came down after Dusty finished his tirade and said to me, "You really started a shitfire here, kid. Good luck tonight." At the time, I had no idea what he was talking about, but gave a smile and a nod just to be polite. I saw Dusty around WCW for the next week; then he was gone.

The Center Stage Theatre had two little locker rooms. One for the stars, one for the extras who didn't have contracts. Before he had gone upstairs to colorfully voice his displeasure about Bischoff, Dusty pointed toward one of the rooms and told me to drop my stuff and take a seat inside. Once news of my arrival had spread through the building, thanks to Dusty's ruckus, Chip Burnham came looking for me to say hello. When he found me relaxing in the extras' locker room, he grabbed my bags and led me into the stars' locker room. At the time, I had no idea that the two locker rooms were divided according to your status in the company, Dusty just pointed and told me to go. There was nobody else in either locker room yet, so I figured I went into the wrong place and Chip was helping me out.

As the afternoon moved along, every top star in the company came strolling into this locker room and they're all looking at me like, *Who the hell is this kid? And what is he doing in our locker room?* But no one actually said anything to me.

And I don't mean they just didn't ask me why I was in their locker room, they didn't say anything to me. Not one word. They pretty much pretended I wasn't there.

Arn Anderson was the last one of the stars to show up, and the only seat left was the one right next to the new kid that no one wanted. He took the seat, introduced himself, and we became friends that day. Boom. That was it, right away. We talked a bit about the business before I had to go out there, then after my match he came over to me and said, "Looks like you got yourself a job, kid." I was thinking, *Holy shit, this is awesome!* I had

Arn Anderson, a wrestler I looked up to for years, complimenting me on my match, basically telling me that I was about to take a huge step in realizing my dream. I also felt that the match went well, that I had accomplished what I came down to Atlanta to do—prove to Eric Bischoff that he should hire me. There was only one problem after the match . . . I couldn't find Eric.

After asking around, I found out that he had already left for the night. Great. I shouldn't have been too surprised because the whole process of the tryout was disorganized and unprofessional.

Eric had called me into his office some time that afternoon to lay out the match. He said I was going to work with some kid named Keith Cole, who I had to put over. That meant I was scheduled to lose. *Win. Lose. Whatever. It all sounds great to me. Let's get it on.* I wasn't there that day to improve my win-loss record; I was there to show them what I could do in the ring. I didn't give a shit who won the match. Eric wished me luck and I went to get ready.

Five minutes after I left his office, I was called back in. This time he said that he'd just been testing me and since I had such a good attitude he'd put me over.

The whole thing was just ridiculous. I had to pay my own way down to Atlanta to prove to them I had talent and he's wasting time pulling goofy tricks to test my attitude.

I show up the next night and have pretty much the same experience. My match was solid, a lot of the boys congratulated me when I came back to the locker room, and Bischoff had taken off before I could speak with him.

Before I left for the hotel that night, someone from the WCW office stopped me to say, "We'll be in touch." Not exactly the contract offer I was looking for.

I didn't hear from anyone that night. It was tough to deal with. I went from being about as high as I can go, with all the boys telling me what a great job I did and that I'd earned a job for sure, to being at a low point thinking nobody in the office cared for my ability enough to call. As I'm literally walking out the door the next morning to catch my flight, the phone rang. It was Bischoff.

After giving me some reason why he didn't talk to me at the building either night, he offered me a deal. Two years, fifty grand a year. Now, that's a good amount of money, but I knew I'd have to move to Atlanta and survive out on the road with that salary. There were a lot of additional expenses I'd be taking on. Plus, it's not like I was bankrupt, working at a dead-end job, living with my parents just to get by. I had a solid job with Gold's. I was managing one of the branches, consulting for others, making good money. It wasn't just a job I was doing until I made it as a professional wrestler; it was the beginning of a great career. If I never made it as a wrestler, that's what I would be doing right now—running a chain of my own gyms. So from a financial perspective, it's not like their offer represented some huge cash windfall over what I was already making. And the work wasn't nearly as stable. I had to voice my concerns.

"I appreciate the offer, but the money's going to be tough. I was kinda hoping for more," I said in another one of those moments where I probably shouldn't have been so forceful with the head of WCW. When he told me he couldn't go over fifty thousand dollars annually, I changed my negotiating tactic.

"Okay then, let's just do a one-year agreement."

"No way. There's no commitment with a one-year deal," he argued.

"Of course there is. It's one full year. Plus, a one-year deal is a win-win for you."

"How you figure?"

"Because at the end of the one year, either you'll see I'm no good and cut me loose, which will save you fifty grand, or you'll want to keep me around because I'm worth it and making money for the company. And if that happens, you'll be happy to pay me more."

"We don't usually do it that way, but okay, why not? It makes sense. You have three months to move to Atlanta, and I'll give you one thousand in moving expenses."

When we hung up, I was stoked. I'd just been hired by WCW. To this day I'm still surprised I had the presence of mind to think this through and negotiate for just a one-year deal so quickly. It would prove to be a great move for me. Of course, that thousand dollars in moving expenses Eric "gave" me came off my salary. So my big bonus turned out to be getting my first paycheck a few days early.

Now that I was in WCW, it was up to me to take advantage of the opportunity. In order to give it my all, I had to make a difficult personal sacrifice before I started.

I'd been dating the same girl for about four years back in New Hampshire. I think everyone's expectation—hers, our families', I guess in a way even mine—was that we'd get married someday. That's just the direction we were heading. So when I officially accepted the offer from WCW, she was all set to move with me. After thinking about it for a few days, though, I told her I wanted to go alone. I was about to throw myself into an unpredictable life in order to chase my dream and it wouldn't have been right for me to bring her along. She wouldn't have known anyone in the city we were moving to, I didn't know how often I'd be around, I didn't know what we'd do for money, I just didn't know what to expect. But it wasn't all for her benefit. I knew when I got down there the only thing I wanted to focus on was wrestling. I didn't want to be distracted from achieving my goals. It was an extremely tough decision, but a sacrifice I had to make.

Surviving the first couple of months in WCW was challenging. Over the course of a few weeks, I went from a guy who rarely left New Hampshire to a guy flying all over the world on tour. I was living on my own in a strange city where I didn't know a single person.

When I was out on the road, I wasn't doing anything right. I was staying in the wrong hotels, eating at the wrong restaurants, and renting the wrong cars. Money was going out much quicker than it was coming in. A good night of sleep meant four hours. To try and fit in with the rest of the boys, I'd go out partying every single night until there was nowhere else to go. That usually meant I'd get in around 5 or 6 A.M., and if I was lucky, which was most nights, I didn't get to sleep until 8. About one of the only things I did right was to stay true to the way I felt about drinking, smoking, and drugs. I never got into any of them. My vice was the women. They were my after-hours indulgence. And boy, did I indulge.

The worst things I was screwing up were my training and nutrition. Out on the road, I was lucky to make it to the gym once a week and eat twice a day. I was trying my damnedest to handle this part of life right when I was back home in Atlanta to make up for it. Unfortunately, Atlanta had its share of the ladies too. These "distractions" took up some time, and I was losing my size as a result of not prioritizing the need to eat and train right when

I was home. When I joined WCW I weighed two hundred sixty-five pounds. By the end of that year I was down to two hundred thirty pounds.

Of all the challenges staring me down, the one that threatened to affect my career the most was that I had pretty much bullshitted my way into the company by telling Bischoff I had five years of experience. I was convinced someone was going to call me on it.

And someone did. Terry Taylor.

One night after working a match with Terry, he pulled me aside in the back and asked how long I'd been wrestling. "About five years," I said without missing a beat.

"Five years? That's a long time. You've been active all that time?"

I don't know what it was, but something in me decided to trust Terry and tell him the truth, that I'd been at this for a little over a year. Instead of getting pissed at me for lying, Terry gave me an opportunity. He invited me to work with him at the WCW Power Plant, their training facility. He offered to teach me the rest of what I needed to know to really make it.

Terry saw me as a kid who was busting his ass out there every night. I didn't know what I was doing, but I was killing myself trying to figure it out. I know he respected that attitude, that he could see how bad I wanted to make it, so he threw me a bone. If I hadn't shown up that day at the Power Plant or strolled in an hour late or gave him an attitude—that would have been it. *Screw you, kid.* When he asked me to meet him at the Power Plant, I answered by asking what time I should show up. And I was there early. I wanted to succeed in the worst way, so I didn't care if he kept me at the Power Plant for six hours that first day. I just didn't care. The only thing I wanted to do was learn. Terry could see that.

It's no different than if I ask a young guy today to meet me at the building early to work on some things. If I ask him to show up at four and he's on time or he's waiting for me when I walk in, I know he wants it. But if he strolls through the door at five and says, "Oh shit, I forgot. Sorry, man," I know where he stands.

Usually I don't need to ask a guy to train with me to figure out how dedicated he is to the business. Just from talking to guys in the locker room I can tell which ones have that burn inside them. I always gravitate toward the ones who do because I want to be with that, I want to be around that attitude. This feeling, this desire to be around guys who share your passion for this business is what got me in with Arn, Ric, Terry, and so many of the other guys in WCW who I had looked up to for so long.

I felt that even after only those two days I was in Atlanta for a tryout, I had gained their respect. At the time it was overwhelming for me. If I was, in any way, becoming one of their peers, well, that was too much to handle.

Arn has told me the reason I was immediately accepted in their group, the way I gained their respect right away, was the same thing I heard from the bodybuilders back in New Hampshire when I was a teenager. They all saw how bad I wanted it. Training in the gym. Becoming a successful professional wrestler. They could see I would bust my ass as much as necessary to get what I wanted. In that Center Stage locker room the day I tried out, when I talked to them about the business, they saw the passion I had for it. They saw how much I wanted it, how much I would give to it, and that made me okay by them.

That's why Terry took all that time out to work with me. He sure didn't have to do it, but he knew I wouldn't throw away the opportunity to learn.

At that point in my career I had a strong physical ability and knew how to do all the moves. I just didn't know when to do them or which ones I should pull off when I wanted a certain result. It was in this area—ring psychology—that Terry and Jody Hamilton, the head trainer at the Power Plant, directed my development. They really put the polish on me as far as my in-ring ability is concerned.

Terry helped me outside the ring as well. He didn't only meet me at the Power Plant to train, he invited me into his home. I'd be over there all the time eating dinner with his wife and children or just relaxing. This gave my life a certain stability. It reeled me in a bit, gave me some discipline. We grew to be close friends.

Thanks to the hectic schedule this business forces you to keep, I don't get the chance to speak with Terry nearly as often as I'd like these days. I miss talking to him on a regular basis. He's a tremendous guy whose opinion and thoughts I respect.

This inability to keep up with friends who aren't with the company is just one of the sacrifices we have to make in order to succeed.

Although I knew I was improving as an all-around wrestler and my matches were getting much better, my actual career as a WCW talent hadn't truly taken off yet. I was still working under the name Terra Ryzing, having some real good matches with different guys, but I still had a way to go before I was anywhere close to being considered a big name.

Ric Flair complimented me after a TV taping one day, saying he could notice an improvement in my matches. He asked if I'd been working with anyone and I told him I'd been training with Terry. Ric suggested I keep at it with Terry because everything was starting to click for me.

WCW gave me only five minutes
to transform from Terra Ryzing
to "the French guy," Jean-Paul
Levesque.

A few weeks later, I got a call from Ric, who was helping with the TV writing at the time, asking me to come down to CNN Center to shoot videos promoting some upcoming matches. I had no idea there was even a possibility that they were going to do promos for me, so I was thrilled knowing they were impressed enough with my development that they were going to start pushing Terra Ryzing. Only, when I arrived, I found out the promos weren't for Terra, they were for my new character: "The French Guy."

A lot of strange shit went on during my time in WCW, but this one ranks right up there with the best of them.

"Do you speak French?" Ric asked when I walked in.

"Sorry?"

"Do you speak French?"

"No."

"How come?"

"How come what? How come I don't speak French? I just don't," I said, having no idea what my inability to speak French had to do with my wrestling career.

"But you've got a French last name."

"I'm from New Hampshire. Everyone has a French surname in New Hampshire because we're so close to Quebec. Levesque is kind of like Smith in French."

"Well, the creative department likes your last name and so they've decided you are now a French guy. You're going to cut promos with a French accent."

"A French accent?"

"And be all pompous and arrogant. Try to take as much heat as possible because you are a bad guy now, too."

With only five minutes to create this new character before we started taping, I was forced to go with pretty much the first thing that came to mind. It turned out to be sort of like a bad impression of Inspector Clouseau. During that first taping, I tried to copy his accent as best I could. By the time I debuted on one of the shows as my new character, I completed the transformation into some kind of Three Musketeers character with the above-the-knee leather boots and French Revolutionary War–style clothes—riding pants, a leather jacket, and my hair in a ponytail.

My wrestling name was changed to Jean-Paul Levesque and the plan was to team me with Lord Steven Regal, a British aristocrat, to form an arrogant European duo, "The Bluebloods."

I was just getting to know Regal at the time, but on a personal level, we hit it off right away. He remains one of my closest friends to this day. This all helped us quickly develop into a solid tag team. Our in-ring chemistry was clicking, and we were driving the fans nuts with our antics.

The only problem was that my one-year contract with WCW was about to expire.

Acting on the advice of Terry Taylor and some of the other guys I had become close with, I contacted World Wrestling Federation to see if they had any interest. To my delight, they did. After negotiating and receiving offers from both Vince and Eric, I decided to sign with Vince despite the lack of a specific financial guarantee, something I had from WCW. He offered me an opportunity I couldn't pass up.

Guaranteed money and working less at WCW made it easy for me to move to World Wrestling Federation.

"I want you to understand what I'm offering you. It's a spot. A good spot. I'm not just bringing you in as another guy. I want to run you through my creative department and do this right. While I don't give guaranteed contracts, I'll give you my word that you'll make more in your first year here than WCW was willing to guarantee you."

That was all I needed to hear. The decision was made.

My last day in the WCW office was a difficult one. I had to meet with Eric to tell him my decision face-to-face.

"Why the hell would you leave here with guaranteed money?" he asked. "Plus, we're cutting out house shows, we're just going to be a TV product. I'm going to give you X amount of dollars to work one or two days a week at the most. How could you have logically looked at these offers and decided that you want to go work three hundred days a year for Vince McMahon at a company that is probably going to file for bankruptcy within the year? How can you look me in the eye and say that's a sound business decision?"

"The things you're selling me as points I should stay is why I'm leaving," I said. "If I stay here, I'm not going to get any better. If I work for Vince, I'm going to be wrestling three hundred days a year in a different city every night against a different opponent every night. It will make me become a great wrestler. And then, if Vince goes out of business in a year, which I highly doubt, you are going to hire me back for a lot more money than you're offering me now because I'll be that much better."

"That's the dumbest shit I ever heard in my life." Then, he basically threw me out of the office.

Before I could get out of the building, Jim Barnett, Kevin Sullivan, and Flair all gave it one last shot to convince me to stay. This was a very tough decision for me anyway, but having these guys I respected so much telling me to stay made it even more difficult. For them to spend all this time trying to get me to stay, telling me how much they wanted me to remain a part of the company—their company—meant so much to me.

When Ric was talking to me about staying that last day, I got all choked up. It was hard for me to walk away from that. He could see my mind was made up, though, and it was time to let me go. As I made my way down one of the hallways toward the exit, I heard Ric call for me to wait up one second. He asked if he could have a word with me in the office. I figured he was about to try one more time to persuade me to stay. He didn't.

"Just between you and me, you go make yourself a star," he told me. "You're doing the right thing. You go wrestle for him like you're capable, and Vince McMahon will make you a star."

I knew this was coming from his heart. All the other shit, giving me reasons why I should stay in Atlanta, that was all his job talking. This message was from the man. He gave up being "the office" in order to be my friend in those final moments.

And he helped me walk out of there completely comfortable with my decision, confident about my future.

As I mentioned when discussing the importance of keeping a training log, eating the right foods is just as vital to achieving your physical goals as lifting weights. You need to fuel your body with the right foods, and enough of them, if you want it to perform at a maximum level.

6. A WORD ON EATING AND NUTRITION

While eating is important, I'm not about to write a diet book here. We all have different body types and different goals, so we need to adjust our diets according to them. The person trying to lose weight should not be eating the same foods as the person looking to add thirty pounds of muscle. We'd need an entire separate book to cover every possible scenario. What I do want to do here is share with you some of my beliefs on eating and nutrition and give you a couple of tips I've picked up over the years.

I'm a believer in a minimum of five or six meals per day, where two of them can be protein shakes. I started this eating schedule, consuming multiple smaller meals, in high school and had tremendous results packing on lean body mass. Eating every two to three hours is the only way to stoke your furnace and keep your metabolism cooking along. If you starve your body for six- or eight-hour stretches, then binge on all sorts of food to squash your hunger, you'll bog down your system. You're asking your body to process and metabolize way too much food at once. As a result, you'll feel sluggish. You sure won't want to hit the gym for an hour at that point.

Eating six small meals daily will keep you satisfied and have your metabolism running high. Plus, with all the energy you'll be expending at the gym, you'll need to consume more food to keep—or get your body up to—the weight you want to be.

You should stick to basic foods like lean red meat, chicken breasts, fresh fish, fresh fruits, potatoes, rice, grains, and green vegetables. A wholesome, balanced diet is the way to go. In each meal try to include meat, a starch, vegetables, and plenty of water. Chicken, a green salad, and rice is a perfect meal. Mix and match dense carbs like potatoes and pasta. Don't get too fancy with it—you'll want to keep it simple enough so you can follow it on a day-to-day basis.

One of the best lessons I learned as a teenage competitive bodybuilder was that it's not necessary to keep the type of diet referred to as "super clean." Basically, what this means is that you are taking in no fat, low carbs, and the perfect amount of protein. You cut the skin off grilled chicken and dab it with a napkin, hoping to sop up any oils that may be on it. You never eat an egg yolk. All your food is steamed, never fried. You will drive yourself crazy trying to do this, and it's just not necessary.

I learned early that I didn't
need a "super-clean" diet
to look and feel good.

If you aspire to be the next Mr. Olympia, then you actually do have to go to this extreme. But if you want to have a healthy body, look good on the beach or playing hoops without a shirt, if you want any of those things, then you don't have to eat like Mr. Olympia. I see guys in our business who drive themselves haywire trying to eat super clean. They'll get in an argument with the guy at Denny's at 2 A.M. because they are convinced he's bullshitting them about their hash browns being steamed. The mental stress they are causing themselves over two lousy grams of fat is so much worse than actually eating the two grams of fat.

I'll never forget the day I learned all of this. It was backstage at a body-building contest that featured Marlon Darton as a guest poser. Marlon, a former Mr. Universe, put on one hell of a show with his impressive physique. And when he got back to the locker room, he started chowing down on a pizza! My jaw dropped and my eyes were bugging out of my head. I couldn't believe what I was seeing. He looked over at me, held up a slice of pizza, and said, "Kid, this is what muscles are made of."

We got to talking, and he set me straight on how I approached diet. He made me see that the way I was eating—dry chicken with no sauce, dry baked potatoes with no butter or sour cream—was absurd for my body type. Admitting that my toughest challenge was putting on weight, Marlon sent me down a totally different path. "For you, you should eat everything under the sun. If you eat a baked potato, put everything on it. Load it up with butter and sour cream. You should be eating as much as you possibly can."

Getting this advice made my life simpler. At that time I was sixteen or seventeen, still living and eating at home with my parents—who were not bodybuilders. My mom made dinner for our whole family, so she wasn't about to make a special dinner just for me. She wasn't going to whip up dry chicken breast with steamed rice and a dry baked potato in addition to the dinner she was making for everyone else. My mom wasn't taking orders.

So after my talk with Marlon, a tremendous strain was lifted off me. Rather than worrying about everything I put in my body, I was like, *Oh I can eat that . . . and a whole shitload of it too!*

You certainly can't afford to gorge on high-fat foods with little other nutritional value all the time and expect your body to look in top shape. But loosening up on what you eat isn't going to kill you. Smearing a little cream cheese on your bagel now and then isn't going to be the end of the world. Just keep in mind that if you have a different body, if you're someone who's prone to carry more body fat, obviously you have a different goal with training and your nutrition routine should reflect that. I don't want you to finish reading this chapter thinking I'm telling you to go and eat a bunch of crap. The lesson to take away is that you have to eat for your body type and your goals.

With everyone constantly on the go these days, planning a proper diet on a daily basis is next to impossible. Let me give you some ways to adapt a healthy eating style to your everyday world.

DON'T WORRY ABOUT EATING SANDWICHES FOR LUNCH

Grab a turkey, chicken, or roast beef sandwich and put any condiment that you want on it. Many bodybuilders will tell you to forget mayonnaise exists because it's too high in fat. Whatever. Don't worry about putting mayo on your sandwich. A tuna sandwich with mayo sure won't kill you.

There are a couple of things you can do to make this lunch better for you nutritionally. Get your sandwich on whole wheat bread and ask the guy behind the counter to put double the meat on your sandwich. They may end up charging you an extra buck or two, but it's worth it. Just make sure you choose leaner meats like turkey or sliced chicken rather than salami or bologna. You should also skip the potato chips and substitute a peach or an apple so that you get some fiber along with the proteins, carbohydrates, and fats from the sandwich.

MAKE IT A PROTEIN SHAKE

Skip the ice cream shakes at In-N-Out or McDonald's and opt for a protein shake. Go with either milk and egg or whey protein powder that you'd buy

Whether at home or on the road, I always find the time to fix myself a protein shake.

at your local nutrition supplement store or supermarket. Mix the shake with milk and eat some fruit with it or use a blender to thicken up the consistency closer to what an ice cream shake is like. I believe you should eat some whole food with supplements to get some real food in your system, so I might eat a bagel or something like that with the shake.

EATING ON THE ROAD

Thanks to a schedule that keeps me on the road over two hundred days out of the year, this area has become my specialty. Charles Glass and one of his partners, noted nutritionist Mike Watson, have given me so much valuable guidance related to eating, but none may have been more important for me than their ability to get me over my fear of fast food. The fact is, you should always go with real food over supplements. So if you have to choose between another protein bar or a stop at Wendy's . . . pull over at Wendy's. Just be careful of what you order.

Chances are, even if you don't have a travel schedule like a WWE Superstar, you often find yourself out on the road, hungry, searching for something to eat. If you know what you're looking for, you can pretty much find something decent to eat at most popular roadside stops.

Gas Stations or 24-Hour Convenience Stores

Buy yourself a big tub of yogurt or a half-gallon container of milk. Supplement that with a package of nuts and a bagel and you're in business for the next three hours.

McDonald's (or Wendy's, Carl's Jr., etc.)

Buy two grilled chicken breast sandwiches and throw away one of the buns. If they run out of chicken for some strange reason, order two double cheeseburgers and throw away one of the buns. This isn't the best source of protein, but it will still give your body what it needs for the next few hours.

Subway

You can get a turkey and cheese sandwich, with double meat, and have yourself a solid meal here. Subway actually has the double meat option on the menu, so take it every time. Keep your protein high and moderate the carbs. That strategy has been instrumental in my most significant physique changes over the past five years. It's not so much the fat content but the carbs you need to worry most about.

Denny's

We're talking about the only place in the Northeast that has been open late at night since I can remember. I'm so tired of Denny's, in fact, that I'm willing to drive an extra five miles to the next exit—even at 3 A.M.—just to *see* if I have other options.

If I can't avoid it, though, there are plenty of good protein choices at Denny's. Egg whites, steak, chicken breasts, and whole eggs. Ask them to cook the eggs without oil and to steam—rather than fry—the hash browns if they can. If not, don't sweat it.

On a Plane

Oh yes, the most difficult spot of all to find healthy food. And most times, you're not going to. That's why I'll usually put two or three sandwiches in a Ziploc bag and bring them with me on the plane. If I'm already on the road before the flight, I'll order a few turkey sandwiches from room service and pack them away. I bought a specially designed briefcase that combines both of my necessities—eating and doing business—into one handy bag. It has a cooler compartment complete with insulation built into it.

Like most of your diet routine, this is all based on planning. I know it can be difficult, but you have to set some time aside to think ahead about your eating. It's just as important as finding time to go to the gym.

MY DAILY DIET PLAN

I usually have my first food intake of the day around 10:30 A.M. right when I get up. My perfect scenario is to then eat every two, two and a half hours from that point until I go to bed early the following morning. Meetings and other obligations make it impossible to achieve that goal sometimes, though. And that's fine, but I draw my limit at three hours. I'll do whatever I need to do to make sure I don't go longer than three hours without eating.

This schedule means I'm usually getting seven food intakes each day. I like to alternate between protein shakes and real food, so every day I'm pretty much going through four protein shakes and three real meals or vice versa.

One of the problems I have is that there comes a point where I just get tired of eating. I get sick of food and can't take in the amount of calories I need. I make up for this by adding essential fatty acids (EFAs) to my protein shakes to up my calorie intake every day.

But there are other reasons why EFAs are important to take. Let me try to explain this without getting too scientific on you. Have you ever heard anyone talk about *good* fat? They were talking about EFAs like omega-3 and omega-6. These fats are considered "good" because they provide support to so many of your body's systems—cardiovascular, reproductive, immune, and nervous. They all benefit from EFAs, but the body can't produce them. That's why it's important to make sure you're getting enough of these EFAs. You can certainly get plenty in some of the foods you eat—salmon, avocado, and nuts, just to name a few—but it might not be a bad idea to pick up some flaxseed or borage oil at your local health food store and drop it in your protein drinks to make sure you're getting the proper amount of EFAs.

Meal #1

I prefer a milk and egg protein shake to whey protein in the morning, but milk and egg isn't as easy to find. The difference is that milk and egg protein is a time-release, slow-to-process protein source, while whey powder burns much faster through the system and is best suited for post-workout meals.

Meal #2

This would technically be considered my breakfast. It's a couple of chicken breasts, six whole eggs, a large serving of oatmeal, and fruit juice.

Meal #3

My second protein shake of the day, once again with the addition of EFAs.

Meal #4

This is my pre-workout meal. I usually have two or three chicken breasts, two or three servings of rice, and two servings of vegetables.

Meal #5

This is my post-workout shake, so I'll usually go with a whey protein shake here. I want something that is high in protein and low in simple carbs.

Meal #6

My final actual meal of the day. I go with either a large steak or a couple of pieces of fish. I'll have smaller portions of rice and vegetables with my meal and add a salad.

Meal #7

Right before I go to bed, I have a milk and egg protein shake. Because it's the longer-lasting protein type, it's the best one to go with before bed to make sure your body is getting what it needs throughout the night.

In one of our first meetings after I officially signed on with World Wrestling Federation, Vince McMahon told me that he liked the character I was doing in WCW and wanted me to bring a lot of its elements with me up north. The biggest change we were going to make was

7. MY WORLD WRESTLING FEDERATION CAREER BEGINS

that I was no longer going to be a Frenchman. Vince was concerned that if they ever wanted to turn me babyface, which meant turn me into a "good guy," it would be immeasurably more difficult to do if I was this over-the-top European guy.

His idea was that I would take that elitist attitude and turn it American. I'd be an aristocrat, a blueblood, someone who came from a life of privilege and made sure you knew it. A lot of people thought Vince created the character as a message to his snobby real-life neighbors in Greenwich, Connecticut, who looked down at him as "the wrestling guy." The story was that having a character with their background on his show, running around acting like an asshole, he was kind of flipping them all off. I never found out if that was for sure, but anything's possible, I guess.

Once we had the idea for my character down, it became a collaborative process with so many people in the office to bring it to life. The creative services department came up with different designs for my outfits. The television studio created vignettes, video ads that ran during the TV shows, promoting my arrival. The marketing department lent their opinions on names. The greatest thing about the company was that they just didn't come up with something and say, "Here, this is your new name and here are your new trunks. Good luck!" They asked for my input and took it into account every step of the way. They made me a part of the creation of what I would become. At the time, I couldn't help but laugh at the differences between their way of creating a new character and the WCW's way of, "Surprise! You're a French guy today!"

Once the look of the character was built, it was completely up to me to make him real. I came up with the bowing, the smug facial expressions, all of that. But long before any of those slight nuances surfaced, I needed to get my body into shape. I'd let my physique slide south as I was leaving WCW. Jean-Paul Levesque had a soft, round look that made it seem like he'd eaten too much French pastry. I knew the couch potato look was not exactly what I was going for with Hunter Hearst-Helmsley.

I needed to have my body looking better in order to credibly support the character I was going to portray. This is a great example of how my career goals shaped my workout routine during a specific time in my life. As a privileged, arrogant jerk on camera, I needed to project an image of perfection. I didn't have to look like an immense bodybuilder; I needed to look in shape. One of the areas I increased my focus for a number of reasons was

"Hunter Hearst-Helmsley" may have felt smug in his debut, but my body was nothing to brag about.

I focused more on cardio than on the weights to get Hunter Hearst-Helmsley into ring shape.

my cardio fitness. For one, it gave me the fit, athletic look I was after. I also had to have the physical ability to wrestle three hundred days a year. The less-intense schedule of WCW was nowhere as demanding, so I could get by. Relating it back to the character, another trait I thought would be important for Hunter Hearst-Helmsley to have was that he'd always appear in control of himself and the situation. I knew it would be difficult to get this image across if I was in the middle of the ring sucking wind after three minutes.

Whether you're taking on a new character to advance your wrestling career or running your first marathon, your workout routine should be shaped by your real-life goals.

When it was time for me to get in the ring as Hunter Hearst-Helmsley, I was certain that I would succeed. The character had been working to an extent in WCW in that it was getting a good heel reaction, so that part of it was a natural transition. And I knew that I had the ability to perform to the level I needed to in the ring.

I was confident, although not overly cocky or arrogant. I knew I was a minnow in the ocean and was respectful of the situation, but at the same time, I knew that when I got in the ring it was my opportunity to go. Some people might argue that I didn't fully back up this belief, because I wasn't an instant success. I didn't come in and—wham, boom—all of a sudden I was the main-event guy. But I don't think I was ready to be.

My career progressed with a deliberate pace at the company. I worked my ass off and was given a step up when I deserved it, but I also made some mistakes and paid the price along the way.

On a personal level, my transition into the company was a smooth one. A lot of the other guys came up to me during my first few weeks and said things like, "We knew you'd be here soon" or "We watched you down in WCW and liked what you did." I know that guys like Shawn Michaels, Kevin Nash, and Scott Hall all went to Vince early in my WCW days and told him they should take a look at me, see what I was doing down there. So in the locker room, among the boys, I had a bit of a buzz going. Especially with those three guys and the 1-2-3 Kid, Sean Waltman. This was the group known backstage as the "Clique."

A few months after starting up with the company, I had my first match with Sean Waltman in Madison Square Garden. It was one of those matches that while it was going on, we could feel how well it was going. You can sense the crowd is into it, reacting with every move. We were one of the first matches that night, and we blew people away. When we got back behind the curtain, Kid went right over to Shawn, Kevin, and a couple of other veteran guys who were huddled around watching and told them, "Damn . . . that guy can go! He's good!" People had such high respect for Sean's in-ring ability that his saying this was a huge endorsement of me. Everyone took notice.

I was at the airport picking up my rental car to start the next tour while Kevin was parked outside, waiting for the other guys to land. He called me over and asked what I was doing. I told him I was just waiting for my car so I could head over to the hotel. "You don't need your own car, jump in with us."

Cutting down on expenses is always a good move, so I threw my shit in their van and we were all pretty much inseparable from that point on.

A lot of the other wrestlers held strong resentment toward the Clique at this time. They thought we had too much influence, were too opinionated and too vocal. I won't argue the point that we were opinionated, because we were. But we didn't have all this influence that people thought we did. We had access to Vince, just like so many others, and we would use that access to pitch our ideas to him. He ended up using a bunch of them, but there were others that he hated. Never did we go to Vince or any of the other agents with an idea and threaten them like, "If you guys don't let us do this, we're all quitting!" Never.

The big thing about the Clique that no one wanted to understand was that we weren't a group of guys who liked causing problems or starting trouble.

We were five guys who really loved the business. We shared a passion for it. When we were on these car rides for hours driving through the middle of nowhere, that was what we talked about—the business. We would spend hour after hour coming up with ideas for different story lines.

You still hear people complain about us to this day, moaning that we used our stroke with the office to our advantage. That's just not true. I remember one time when I was still very new, Vince and Gerry Brisco flew out to Indianapolis to meet the five of us and talk about the company. Vince was at a point where he wanted to overhaul the business and was interested in our opinions on what exactly he should do. I was so new at this point that I didn't want to sit in the meeting because I didn't feel that I'd earned the right yet. Vince came over to me as I was walking away and said, "Get in here, you're a part of this too. You seem like you have a good head for this stuff and I want your opinion." To open the meeting, he handed out the complete talent roster and asked, "If this were your company, who would you want on your team and why?"

The funniest part about the whole scene was that a lot of the people that hated us the most were some of the first people we told Vince we wanted on our team. "I think he's got it. He's an asshole, but he can play on our team any day." Guys that shit on us the most, that told everyone we were the worst thing in the history of the business—we didn't let that cloud our professional judgment. We didn't go after them because of that. We were all in it for the business, basing all of our feelings and opinions only on what was best for the business. It was during this meeting in Indianapolis that we all started discussing the idea of moving away from the cartoons and toward more reality-based characters. Once the company fully went in that direction in the late nineties, it revolutionized the business.

Vince has told me a million times over the years, "So many people shit on the Clique, and their complaining caused a lot of problems. But if I'd had a whole roster of guys with the same attitude and passion as the Clique, I'd have no issues."

While I was having a blast with the guys backstage and on the road, I was about to make a decision that gave my character a huge boost and earned me respect with the office. The decision might not seem like much. Quite simply, all I did was agree to do my job to the best of my ability.

One of the angles we had going at the time was Henry Godwinn as a farmer who'd throw a bucket of pig shit on his opponents at the end of matches. Henry and his slop bucket were such a hit with the fans that it turned him from a bad guy, what we call a heel in the business, into a babyface. Right before he fully made the turn, Vince wanted Henry to work with a wrestler named Adam Bomb.

Adam was a guy that Vince really got behind, giving him a gimmick and pushing him pretty hard. So they wanted him to work with Henry one night where the finish would be Henry dumping the slop all over him to start a big angle between them. Adam was reluctant at first, but they finally convinced him. They told him to make sure to take it in the face because it would generate the best reaction from the fans and really get them behind Henry. When the time came, Adam turned over and took it on his back. This pissed off the office. He just wouldn't do it the right way. And they canned him shortly after. He was just one of those guys in the business who liked to know that the guys in the gym thought he was cool and that meant there's no way some other guy was throwing pig slop at him, embarrassing him on television.

You still see this attitude around the locker room today. It's one of the biggest problems in the business. There are too many guys who are worried that when they walk into their hometown gym on Tuesday morning, their lifting buddies are going to laugh at them because of something they did on *Raw* the night before. You've got guys more concerned with keeping up this cool image among their pals than they are with entertaining the fans and making a ton of money doing it.

I'll give you a guy who's on the other side of that: William Regal. Over the years, a lot of the things he's done on that show—like being tricked into drinking pee or joining the "Vince McMahon Kiss My Ass Club"—ninety percent of the guys in our locker room would have told the creative team there's no way they're doing any of that. But not Regal. His response is always something like, "Oh, that's bloody great!" He knows the types of reactions these angles will get and as a result, he's one of the most entertaining characters on our show the last few years. This attitude is what separates the guys that are truly great in our business from the guys whose success has a limit. It totally blows my mind that more people in our business don't have this attitude. You think Kurt Angle ever turned down an idea because it was too embarrassing? Here's a legitimate Olympic Gold Medalist who's let us make fun of his gold medals, make fun of his being an Olympian. He doesn't care. Nothing is off limits. He knows this is entertainment, and that's one of the main reasons he's such a big star.

So a few months after the Adam Bomb thing went down, they asked me what I thought about working with Henry. I was like, "All right! That'll be great!" Don't get me wrong, I wasn't looking forward to jumping into a pile of pig shit during the Pig Pen match we had. I knew I'd be getting pig slop everywhere on my body, but I also knew the fans would go nuts for it. I could have gone into the match, let Henry throw me down in it once, stand up going, "Ewwwww . . . ewwwwww . . . this is gross," and end it right there, or I could really put on a show. And that's what I decided to do. We had Henry drop me facedown in a pile of shit—it was all over me—then I fell in it again, started throwing it all over the place, and fell down a couple more times. I really got into it. We wanted to entertain the fans, really give them an unbelievable payoff to the series of matches we'd had up to that point. And we succeeded. They were laughing their asses off the entire time.

This angle between Henry and me went on for like six months, and the fans loved every minute of it. On a personal level, it remains one of my fonder memories. Sure, I ended up having to throw out six sets of gear because the slop ruined them, but the whole story line was so much fun to do, and the fans had such a blast with it too, that I wouldn't trade that experience for anything.

While the story line was going on, I knew that some of the other young guys were laughing behind my back about getting the pig shit thrown in my face for six months. But I didn't care one bit because here's what else I knew: I was out there having a good match every night. While they were behind the curtain giggling away at me, I was out there blowing the roof off Madison Square Garden. There were eighteen thousand people going wild when Henry started throwing me around in that slop and I was rolling all over the place in it, playing it up. I didn't care who was making fun of me backstage, I wasn't doing it for their benefit. I was covered in pig shit because I knew it would get a reaction every night, and to me, getting a reaction one way or the other is what this business is all about. I knew the connection I was making with the fans during this time was leading me somewhere.

Not only was Hunter Hearst-Helmsley becoming a bigger heel in the eyes of the fans, but my positive attitude through all of this made an impression on Vince and the agents.

I knew rolling around in pig shit would one day take me to the top.

My career continued up as a result. I kept on gaining steam with the fans, and the creative team was giving me a big push toward the top. They had me scheduled to win the *King of the Ring 1996* and follow that with a series of matches with Shawn Michaels that would result in a championship bout. The plan was all set.

About two weeks prior to *King of the Ring*, we had a house show at Madison Square Garden. It was a live event that wasn't for television; we

I was supposed to win *King of the Ring* in 1996, but a screwup on my part delayed that a year.

were only performing for the people in the arena. It was also Kevin and Scott's last night with the company. The two had signed on with WCW as the *Monday Night Wars* really started to escalate.

As it worked out, the four members of the Clique who were working the show—Shawn, Kevin, Scott, and I—were involved in matches with one another. I beat Scott in a vicious brawl and Shawn took Nash in a Cage match to finish off the night. Shawn asked Scott and me to come back into the ring at the end of their match for a final photo of the four of us, who were like brothers.

I don't know how Shawn explained it to Vince beforehand, but when we all got together, things went in a different direction. It was an emotional night. There was hugging and backslapping and smiling. The four of us remained in the ring, our hands locked as we raised our arms in triumph.

This clearly broke the code of secrecy in our business. Moments earlier, the four of us were all trying to pulverize one another and now we were revealing the truth—that we were actually the best of friends. The fans at the show that night loved it, but a lot of people from the office were pissed.

And I could see why they were. Even though the company had already admitted it was "entertainment," this was the first public display proving that label true. Not to mention that we did this in Madison Square Garden, long considered our company's home arena, and this was a huge deal.

We did pull back the proverbial curtain of our business a bit and revealed our magic. But that wasn't our intention. We didn't set out to deliberately attack the code of secrecy that surrounds our business. At first, Vince didn't have a problem with what we did. I think there was a part of him that respected it because he saw that it was never meant to be more than two guys saying good-bye to two other guys they had shared a lot of great times with over the years. An emotional good-bye between four guys who became brothers traveling up and down the road. Despite understanding all of this, he still had to lay down a punishment.

The problem was that Kevin and Scott were leaving, and as the World Champion and biggest draw in the company, Shawn was untouchable. That meant the entire fallout would land squarely on me. I didn't complain, because I should have known better. It was a major screwup that was going to cost me dearly.

Vince didn't fire me, though. He knew that as the youngest guy, I definitely didn't come up with the idea; I didn't lead the other three into it. I also think he believed that I was a valuable performer, someone he didn't want to hand back over to Bischoff.

When we met in his office about it, Vince offered me the opportunity to get out of my contract and go to WCW to be with my friends. I told him I came from there and no way did I want to go back. So he explained to me with brutal honesty what that meant for my immediate future.

"You're not going to win *King of the Ring*," he said. "You're not getting involved in a program with Shawn. Your career will get put on hold for a bit. You're going to have to learn to eat shit and like the taste of it."

The only thing I asked Vince during our meeting was that I get his assurance that the incident was done. I apologized and told him I respected his decision to punish me, but I needed to know that one day he was going to feel that I'd taken enough punishment and when that day came he would give me another opportunity to shine. I needed him to tell me that this was something he could get past.

"Yes, this is over right now. You have to do your punishment, do your time, but between you and me personally, this issue is over. Done. Forgiven."

I took his word, accepted my punishment, and got ready for the day when my opportunity would come again.

One spot that seems to cause the most trouble for a lot of people is their abs. It also happens to be the spot those people are most anxious to tone up. If you're serious about being fit, there's a good chance that one of your first goals is to get that hard-to-attain "six pack."

8. TRAINING YOUR ABS

The main reason abs are a difficult muscle group to sculpt is that you can't spot-reduce the fat that's covering the abs. To get that chiseled look you're after, you'll need to burn the fat covering your abs through cardio exercise and a relatively low-fat diet. If neither of these options appeals to you, your only other hope is that you were blessed with the genetic tendency to be lean and develop muscle in that area.

Of course, you'll need to do ab exercises in addition to the cardio and low-fat diet. You should be leery of those cable infomercials that promise you can get ripped abs in five minutes by strapping an apparatus to your stomach while you sit around and read a magazine. It's bullshit. But hitting abs only twice each week is fine. If you hit them hard, you certainly don't need to train abs every day.

I like to work on them at the end of the chest/biceps workout, as I'm not as tired and mentally depleted as I am at the end of my back or leg days. Then I'll just go with how I feel other days of the week to see where I can fit in my second one. If I can get in only one abs session during the week, though, I certainly don't flip out.

I work the abs only twice a week, but I know it's integral to my entire routine.

My abs work usually consists of some basic exercises like crunches and slant-board leg raises for 3 sets of 10–30 reps.

Remember, with this muscle, you are not trying to build up size, as you are with all your other body parts. The objective for your abs is to tone the muscles. The best way to do this is through exercises that contract the abs as you complete each exercise—a slow, precise movement, exhaling as you contract and pause for a count of 1, 2, 3.

The exercises you see in the photos on the color pages 44–48 will help you chisel the rectus abdominis—the long, vertical muscle that runs from the rib cage to the pubic bone. One other secret is to hold your stomach in whenever possible. As you're walking around during the day, contract the muscles in your stomach. This is a matter of posing and posture. If you always allow your stomach to extend outward, it will eventually become distended.

Even if you don't immediately achieve the "six pack," don't give up on abs training. It's such an integral part of your overall routine because it strengthens the core of your body—lower abs and lower back. The core is the center of your body, and all overhead movements, such as presses and pulldowns, depend on keeping the core sound and in synch with the high-impact body parts like chest, arms, back, and legs.

It all starts with your body's core.

For detailed instructions on the exercises in this chapter, see color pages 44–48.

My punishment went on for six months, a year—I don't know exactly because it wasn't like I was called back in the office one day and told "Okay, we're putting your career back on track." When I look back on the whole thing—and this is something I never would have seen

9. FROM DX TO THE GAME

while it was going on—I'm actually glad this all went down the way it did. I now know that I wasn't a mature enough performer to become a main-event guy at that time. The punishment forced me to take a bit longer to get to the top, but I learned so much during that period. I learned how to truly be a man in the business. The time allowed me not only to improve my work in the ring even more, but also to pick up knowledge outside the ring, on the business side of our industry.

I was in a much better position to take advantage of the opportunities presented to me when the punishment was over. It prepared me for the rest of my career. When Shawn and I eventually started D-Generation X (or DX), a group we formed on our programs that was based on the Clique, I was in a much better position to capitalize on it. When Shawn split and I took over DX, I was way ready to be in that spotlight, to lead that group. Then when DX had run its course, I was damn ready to take the next step. I was ready to get that great run in as a heel, which led me to being World Champion and all that comes with it. It all progressed at the right pace.

Here's how it started: After it had become obvious that the office was no longer interested in holding me back for what I'd done at Madison Square Garden, I had two ideas in the works. I was looking for a bodyguard for my current character, and at the same time, Shawn and I were trying to pitch the idea of a new faction to Vince. The faction that would become D-Generation X.

One night after a show in Springfield, Massachusetts, Shawn and I headed over to the hotel to check in for the night. We noticed Jack Lanza talking to someone at the bar as we made our way to the elevators and decided to stop for a quick hello. Although you wouldn't have imagined it from her physique, we could see it was a woman as we got closer. Jack jumped up and yelled out to us before we even spoke. "Well all right! Here they are . . . These are the two guys you should really be talking to." He was looking to get out of the situation, and with that line he had successfully pawned this woman over on us. In a few months, the entire world would know her as Chyna, the Ninth Wonder of the World. She would become one of the hottest things in the entire industry for a few years.

The first thing you noticed about her was that she was huge. Not fat, muscular. We found out that she was supposed to meet Jack over at the building with her resume, but ended up missing him so she tracked him down to the hotel. She was trying to get a job as a wrestler. When we heard this, Shawn and I nodded at each other, knowing the same exact thing was

Chyna was the "Ninth Wonder of the World," but she was even more impressive in the gym.

going through each of our minds . . . *Here's my new bodyguard.* We had her resume and told her we'd pass it around.

We pitched the idea to Vince the next day, and he hated it. "That's just stupid," was pretty much the way he put it at first. "Nobody is going to want to get their ass kicked by a girl."

"But think about it, this is cutting-edge, it's new. No one's ever even thought of this, much less done it," we argued. Vince wasn't having any of it.

Shawn and I wouldn't let up, though. We bugged Vince about it constantly for a couple of weeks. During this time, I'd gotten to know Chyna a little bit. She lived near me, so when I was home I met her at the gym to train. I needed to make sure she wasn't a complete ding-dong before I kept working behind the scenes to bring her into the company. I remember the first day we worked out together at Gold's Gym back up in New Hampshire, we hit chest and started with a warm-up set of 135 pounds on the bench press.

She was cool with that, and I was impressed that a woman could handle so much weight on a warm-up set. We kicked it up to 225 for the next set, and again she had no trouble whatsoever. Then it was on to 275, and she was barely breaking a sweat; it was no harder for her than it was for me. After that I kind of put it on her to make the call of how much weight we'd add. She suggested going all the way up to 315.

Now, to be honest, I was not thinking about going anywhere near that weight—I was still recovering from the last set.

She stepped up first and whacked out two perfect reps. I was really under the gun now because I wasn't sure that I could get two reps at that weight. It was a potentially humiliating situation to deal with. I barely squeezed two out, tried to do a third to make it look good, but she had to pull the bar off me. When I got up, I started holding my shoulder and said to her, "Yeah, my shoulder's been bugging me lately, so I didn't want to push it there on that last rep." I immediately started viewing her as my equal in the gym.

The next time we were up in Massachusetts for a show, Vince called me into his office when I got to the building. He wasn't in the mood for small talk. "Shawn is injured and needs to take some time off. He's going to hand over the title," he said as I walked in. "This show is going to suck. It's the biggest downer in the world. I need to have something big in the beginning of the show that'll be an incredible high for the fans. I need you to lose the Intercontinental title to Rocky Maivia."

"Okay, whatever you need me to do."

"Thanks. And I'll tell you what . . . I'll let you try the thing with the woman. But she's totally your responsibility. If she turns out to be a flake, it's on you."

Shawn went out in front of the cameras later that night and gave his infamous "I've Lost My Smile" speech, I lost the Intercontinental Championship to a newcomer named Rocky Maivia, and we started putting together plans for Chyna's official entrance into World Wrestling Federation. Of course, Rocky Maivia went on to become The Rock—the WWE Superstar with whom I have worked more than anyone else, selling out arenas all over the world, having some of my most memorable matches. No one would have dreamed it at the time, but this night in Massachusetts, which had trouble written all over it, was actually setting our company up for some of its greatest success over the next few years.

Like I said, this was all happening at the same time Shawn and I really started to push the idea of a new faction to Vince. The idea actually started back with Sean, Kevin, and Scott. We had wanted to use the Clique on the show. The business was changing, and we all knew it was changing. One of the things we mentioned to Vince that day in Indianapolis was that we had to get away from cartoons and goofy gimmicks to start becoming more realistic. We needed to be great athletes first, and the rest of it would take care of itself. The whole Clique mystique had become so prominent with the fans—there were Clique signs at every arena—that we wanted to capitalize on it. We didn't want to use the name "The Clique," but the concept behind the angle was rooted in reality. A group of guys who had a good time being around one another and had each other's back every step of the way. Sort of like the Four Horsemen, only with our unique twist on it. Vince didn't like the idea. "Groups never work out, they're never as big as the single guy."

We kept bugging him and bugging him over the years, even after all the other guys took off, and I guess we eventually just wore him down. After Shawn returned, we went to him with a different slant on the idea one day and he told us, "Okay . . . fine . . . we'll start working toward it in a month or so." And the rest is history.

The trio of Shawn, Chyna, and me morphed into D-Generation X, a bunch of, well, degenerates whose arrogance and sophomoric antics made us the hottest thing in sports entertainment not named Stone Cold Steve Austin. Our appearances on the show were always surrounded by controversy. The USA Network wasn't thrilled with some of the things we did out there on live television; in fact, they threatened to throw us off the air. But the fact was undeniable: ratings shot up when we were on. They could never follow through on their threats. Due to DX, we started appealing to a younger, hipper crowd. DX references showed up in movies, on television shows, in magazines. Eddie Murphy was telling people, "Suck it!" in his movies, and

Fans ate up the *Raw* attitude Shawn Michaels and I gave the company with D-Generation X.

in just about every football game you watched, the "Crotch Chop" was part of a touchdown celebration. The business had entered the mainstream in a way we hadn't seen since the mid eighties. It was hard to imagine things going any better for the group. Then, Shawn decided he couldn't go on with his back in the condition it was. He was ready to retire.

After losing the title to Steve Austin at *WrestleMania XIV,* Shawn walked away and many people thought DX would disappear with him.

But I wouldn't let it. I was ready to take over. Everything I had been through up to this point in my career had prepared me to lead this group to even greater heights. When we first started DX, I couldn't have handled the responsibility. I wasn't ready for it. Shawn needed to be our leader, letting me excel in the background. And that helped me. Helped me under-

Raw took no prisoners.

stand what needs to get done as the leader. As the guy who is most responsible for the success—or failure—of a whole group.

With the returning Sean Waltman (then competing in our company as X-Pac) and the New Age Outlaws (Road Dogg Jesse James and Bad Ass Billy Gunn), D-Generation X rose to levels of popularity that, at times, were mind-boggling to me. It was bigger than anything the business had seen in a long time.

Not only were we ripping the roof off every building we went to, we were having a blast doing it. Of all the stunts we pulled during this time, our "raid" of WCW is my all-time favorite. Yeah, it was hilarious, but better than that was how secretive the entire thing was. It was literally only me, one of our writers, Vince Russo, and Vince McMahon who knew what was going on. The rest of DX didn't even know what they were doing until we pulled up to the building that night.

The reason the whole deal came about was that WCW kept booking shows right near ours. The competition between the two companies had escalated into a nasty and at many times personal battle. Nothing was off-limits. There was this period of time when we'd have a show scheduled for a town, we'd be two months out, and all of a sudden we'd find out that WCW announced that they were putting on a show right down the street either that week or a week before. It started to really piss us off.

The week before a show in Roanoke, we were having a conference call to go over some of the creative planning for the event—I had started to help out a little bit with the booking. After someone on the line reminded us that WCW was putting on *Nitro* a few miles away in Norfolk, I blurted out, "Damn! I wanna go over there right in the middle of their show and . . . I don't know . . . do something." I was just so pissed at the situation that I had to say something. I didn't really mean it; I wasn't expecting to go over to *Nitro.*

Vince Russo called me up very early the next morning. "I was thinking about what you said yesterday and it got me thinking. What if we did do something like that?"

I actually had no idea what he was talking about at first. I had made the comment out of frustration and didn't give it a second thought after I hung up the phone the day before. Russo reminded me what I said, and I was immediately on board. We started planning it right away.

When Billy and Road Dogg walked into the building the next day, the first thing out of Dogg's mouth was, "Why's there a jeep with a cannon sticking out of it in the parking lot?"

"That's for us. We're gonna do a gimmick tonight," was all I offered. They pressed me for more, but I wanted Vince McMahon to be the one to tell them because I knew they would think I was bullshitting them. Even coming from Vince, they didn't buy it. We had to spend quite a while convincing them we weren't pulling a joke.

So we went over to the building where WCW was putting on their show to film our "raid." We had the jeep, we were decked out in camouflage, we'd brought signs, bullhorns, all sorts of stuff. Basically, we just made jokes and talked shit about WCW—and the fans ate it up. We tried to get into the building, but they wouldn't let us in, which made no sense if you think about it. Before we left to do it and were going over what we should do when we got there, someone asked Vince what we should do if they didn't let us in the building. He was so confident that we wouldn't have to worry about it that he almost didn't want to waste any time thinking about it. As he put it, "Which wrestling show would you watch, the one that has none of them on it or the one that has all of them on it?" And he had a great point. Every sports entertainment fan in the country would have flipped over to their show when we walked out on camera. Not letting us in the building or on their show was a great indication of how stupid many of the folks running WCW at the time were.

We kind of had an idea as we taped the piece that day that it was going to be big, but we didn't fully understand the response it was going to get that night when it aired and in the weeks immediately after. Even though we were getting some cheers because the stuff we were doing was so funny, so clever that people couldn't help but show their appreciation, we were officially heels at the time of the raid. But that stunt put an end to that. We became total babyfaces to the fans at that point.

We flourished in that role for a while, but in early 1999 I knew I had achieved more than I could've dreamed with D-Generation X and it was time for me to take another step. My plan was to turn on DX and ditch the good-guy image I had built up over the last few months. I wanted to turn into the biggest, meanest, most intense wrestler in the business.

Just like before when I came into the company, this meant I had to transform my body to meet the image I wanted to present. I was about to make a full character transformation—from the good-time leader of DX to a psychopathic pulverizer—and I needed to look the part. I needed to dedicate myself to an ultimate training program.

What most people don't understand is that I didn't pack on all this new weight and muscle to achieve the goals I had. I worked even more closely with Charles Glass and embraced a program that focused more on cutting up the muscle I had rather than packing on new weight. I concentrated on my diet, ate real clean. I'm not embarrassed to admit that I had gotten a bit pudgy toward the end of DX, and that was never going to fly with the new character I wanted to portray. I had to drop my body fat percentage down, knowing that would give me the lean, ripped look I wanted. The change wasn't as dramatic as people want to think it was. I didn't gain thirty pounds or anything like that; I just got leaner.

This is yet another example of a time in my life when my workout routine was shaped by my life goals. I cannot stress this point enough: training can help you achieve your goals, regardless of what they are.

Once I had my body lean and looking closer to how I needed it, I started making other subtle changes—cutting my hair and wearing it wet, growing a beard, going back to short trunks in the ring.

With my total look now changed, it was time for the next stage in my career to take off.

The Game was on.

In a perfect world I'd train five days each week—one body part per day—with the exception of pairing up biceps and triceps in one arm-blasting session. In the real world of limited time and constant travel, though, I can train only four days each week.

10. TRAINING YOUR SHOULDERS AND TRICEPS

I worked to structure a schedule that was realistic, one that took into account everything else I've got going on and would allow me to maximize my time in the gym to build size and strength.

The exact schedule varies somewhat from week to week. The order of body parts and specific exercises depends on what part of my physique I'm prioritizing at that time. If I need to work on my shoulders, for instance, I'll start the training week with a full-throttle shoulder session.

Let me give you an example of what my typical week looks like in the gym. One thing to keep in mind when looking at this schedule is that an off day for me doesn't mean I'm kicking back on the couch with my feet up and the remote in my hand. I'm traveling, wrestling, or even both. My constant wrestling schedule is why I don't do cardio in the gym. I get more than enough in the ring. The important thing you need to understand is that everyone has to take days off from going to the gym.

MONDAY: Off from gym

TUESDAY: Shoulders/triceps

WEDNESDAY: Legs

THURSDAY: Off from gym

FRIDAY: Back/rear delts

SATURDAY: Chest/biceps

SUNDAY: Off from gym

Now that you see what muscles I'm working when I'm in the gym, you need to understand *how* I'm working them.

VOLUME

Except where I say otherwise, I do 4 sets for every exercise I mention throughout the rest of the book. The first set is a warm-up set, where the only thing you should be concerned with is your form. It should be perfect. You're basically getting your body used to completing the exercise, so don't even think about how much weight you're working with for this set. When I work through my warm-up set with something like barbell presses, I only use the bar and very little weight.

The next 3 sets are your working sets. A warm-up set builds form, a working set builds muscle. You should not work with the same amount of weight and complete the same number of reps for each of your working sets. What I do is break them down into light, moderate, and heavy sets, and do each one to failure. When I'm feeling good and working with a partner I trust, I usually have him help me out on a forced rep or two after I reach failure.

I use a weight on the second set that's light enough to let me squeeze out 12–15 reps, and then I raise the weight for the third set, with the goal of hitting the 10–12 range. My fourth set is the one where I really blow it out, striving for maximum growth and stimulation on the muscle. I jack the weight up even higher and look to get out anywhere from 6 to 8 reps before I reach failure.

I move at a quick pace between the first 3 sets, but I take a two- or three-minute break before my final set to make sure my body is totally ready for what I'm about to put it through.

Like I mentioned back in Chapter 4, sometimes you may need to change your routine a bit to keep it fresh. The variations I already told you about are ways to shake things up from set to set, but when I'm in need of a more drastic overhaul, I change the number of reps I do for two weeks straight. I go for two weeks where I lift 15–20 reps across the board and then go the next two with 6–8 reps before I get back to my usual routine. When I do this, I drop the weight down during the higher rep cycle and pick it back up for the lower reps.

My shoulders take a severe pounding in this business, so it's one of the most important muscle groups for me. On this day I'll concentrate on the front and medial deltoids. I'll hit the rear deltoid when I train my back muscles.

I start out by warming up the body's core temperature with ten minutes on a stationary bike. This cranks up the metabolic rate and prepares your target muscles to fill with blood.

DELTOID EXERCISES

Deltoid Exercise #1: Front Military or Dumbbell Press

You could also do behind-the-neck presses here, but some tend to stay away from those. They place much more stress on your easy-to-injure rotator cuff than the front military or dumbbell press.

Deltoid Exercise #2: Lateral Raise

The lateral raise, also known as the side lateral, targets the medial deltoid. Building up this muscle is important because it'll widen up your shoulders. Aside from looking great on their own, thick shoulders will make your waist appear smaller, giving you an overall lean look and your upper body that V shape that so many bodybuilders are after.

Deltoid Exercise #3: Dumbbell Front Raise

This is an effective front-delt crusher that troubleshoots my specific shoulder deficiencies. Though my front delts come up with ease, I'm still troubled by a flat area between my front and side delts that the military dumbbell press doesn't address. This is the only exercise that's able to isolate that one lagging spot in my delt complex.

Deltoid Exercise #4: Dumbbell Shrug

I finish up the shoulder workout with dumbbell shrugs to target the trapezius muscles (the traps).

I like pairing up the triceps with shoulders because they are both pushing muscles. Basically, the exercises I do for them are all about me pushing the weights, not pulling anything toward my body. This means my triceps are also getting a pump while I'm doing shoulder work.

TRICEPS EXERCISES

Triceps Exercise #1: Triceps Pushdown

This exercise is going to hit the horseshoe-shaped muscle that is the triceps. It gives the muscle a great outline and definition.

Triceps Exercise #2: Lying Triceps Extension

This one is the real mass builder of your triceps exercises. Often called "skull crushers" because you are literally bringing the bar down inches from your head, it's the best way to pack meat onto your triceps.

TRIPLE H

There are really a bunch of different triceps exercises you can do in most gyms, but you don't need to do more than two different exercises during any one session. When you want to change up the exercises, you can substitute dumbbell French presses for the skull crushers. Dips, either on parallel bars or behind-the-back, and close-grip bench presses are some other good options.

One thing you can also do with triceps exercises that you shouldn't do with too many other muscle groups is scale it down to only 2 sets. Every time I'm in the gym, I adjust my routine to how I feel during a workout. As it gets later in my triceps work, I may feel like it's best for me to skip the warm-up and light sets and just focus my intensity on the moderate and heavy sets.

The only triceps exercise you can never skip the warm-up set to get your form down is the dumbbell French press. Because you're asking your shoulders to go through an unnatural motion for them—bringing the dumbbell behind your head and stretching it down as far as it can go before extending it skyward—you need to get your form down perfectly on this one or you run a high risk of injury. Tearing your triceps muscle by jumping right into heavy poundages with this exercise is relatively easy to do. Not only is that extremely painful, but it'll also keep you out of action—and the gym—for quite a while. Just what we want to avoid.

For detailed instructions on the exercises in this chapter, see color pages 1–13.

Once I was fully established out on my own, things took off. I was quickly becoming the number one heel in the business and spent most of the summer having a string of awesome matches with Stone Cold Steve Austin, who was still the top babyface. The battles picked up as we

11. THE McMAHON-HELMSLEY ERA

headed toward *SummerSlam*, where we had a Triple Threat match with Mick Foley.

Although we put on one hell of a show for the fans at that Pay-Per-View, the following night was a historic one for me. It was the culmination of years of hard work. All the hours training in the gym. All the time spent busting my ass at Walter's. All the nights spent driving for hours to get from one independent show to the next. It all became worth it on August 23, 1999— the night I first won the WWE title.

Winning the championship is obviously every wrestler's ultimate dream, so when I achieved it, I was ecstatic. It was such an honor for me. Not only because I had this championship title, this tangible reminder that I accomplished a major goal, but I was humbled by what it meant. The company didn't put the title on me just to transition it to someone else. They wanted me to have a long-term run with the championship. By making this decision, they were recognizing me as a top guy—a guy who would serve as the face of the company, represent us to the public.

That's all part of what being the WWE Champion means. It's more than just defending the title once a week on TV. And to trust this responsibility to someone who was a bad guy on the program . . . well, that just wasn't really done. Some people in the office resisted the idea, but fortunately, they were in the minority.

With all my enemies on the show gunning for me once I had the title, I lost it along the way and started up an angle with Vince McMahon to get it back. The story line was that as the "good guy" owner, Vince hated it that such an evil son of a bitch was his champion. And as the evil son of a bitch, I hated it that Vince was a "good guy" owner. We went at it for weeks, tearing up every crowd we went in front of.

At the same time, Vince's daughter, Stephanie, was involved in a major angle on the program as well. Vince Russo had this idea to put on a wedding, so they started a story line where one of the Superstars, Test, would get romantically involved with Stephanie, eventually asking her to marry him. With the wedding announced and weeks away, Russo left for WCW. And no one knew his exact plan to finish off the wedding and transition Steph and Test as a married couple into the show.

The whole thing was up in the air for a while. It was such a major part of our programming, so just dropping it without an explanation was not an

Becoming WWE Champion was not only a
dream come true, but an honor for me to
represent the company.

option. They went so far as to come up with little swerves in the story to postpone the on-screen nuptials while they figured out an ending satisfying enough to the entire story line. There was this one thing they did where Steph got amnesia after she was hit in the head with a garbage can. She couldn't remember who Test was for a few shows, so he had to work to convince her that they were about to be married. This trick bought a lot of time.

With hundreds of suggestions coming in from every possible source, but none receiving overwhelming support, the creative team decided to just move ahead with a regular wedding and play out their marriage for a little bit until something could be figured out for the long term.

You have to understand that at this time pretty much everyone in the company was working on this issue. It was on everybody's mind, *What do we do about the wedding?* Someone said to me backstage at one of the shows, "They should have this crazy swerve where she ends up admitting she's in love with someone else and marries him or something." I thought, *You know, that's not a bad idea.*

Two weeks before the wedding was scheduled to finally take place, it hit me. *It should be me who marries her!* I was in the middle on this hot angle with Vince, so I couldn't think of anyone else on our roster that would have made more sense than me at the time. This was his only daughter, his most precious angel. I didn't think there was a story that would have been better than having the guy who Vince hated more than anyone else turn around and marry her just to piss him off.

I thought the idea out all the way before presenting it to Vince. I decided that we weren't going to turn it to where Steph admitted she was in love with me out of the blue. Oh no. I was going to drug her at her bachelorette party and trick her into marrying me. Vince loved the entire idea and decided to do it right away. We already had a match with one another scheduled for the next Pay-Per-View, so we wanted to work in this latest twist somehow. We added a stipulation to the match that if I won, I'd get a shot at the title, but if I lost, I'd have the marriage annulled so he could have his daughter back. This stipulation was actually our way out of the wedding. We thought we had come up with a great idea that would deliver one hell of an emotional payoff at the actual wedding ceremony, while at the same time give us a way to put the whole marriage behind us for good.

But something funny happened on the way to the match. The night after I showed the world the video of me drugging Stephanie and dragging her into the wedding chapel, the fans turned on *her*. Here was this poor, innocent girl who was completely tricked into marrying some asshole who hated her father, and the fans blamed *her*. The fans already didn't really like the prim-and-proper perfect little daughter Steph was portraying, so this gave them even more of a reason to rally against her. We thought there was a slight chance the fans would have a negative reaction toward her in all of this, but we never saw the passion and the quickness with which they would turn on her. And they were merciless that night. Screaming at her, "Slut! Slut! Slut!"

Witnessing this reaction, we knew we had something incredible, so we went with it. We decided to seal her fate as a full-fledged heel at the Pay-Per-View. Toward the end of the match, I'm down, helpless in the corner, when Vince is about to reconfigure my face with my very own sledgehammer. Before he can bring it down on me, Steph rushes into the ring. She pleads with him to let her do it. Wanting to allow his daughter momentary retribution over the man who ruined her life, Vince hands over the sledgehammer. I'm in front of her, too beaten and exhausted to defend myself, but she just can't hit me. Vince is telling her to get on with it. "Do it, Stephanie!

Stephanie McMahon betrayed her own father at *Armageddon 1999* to be with me, even though we barely knew each other.

Hit him! Destroy him for what he did to you!" But she's not moving. I finally get up and slowly take the hammer away from her. Then I use it to unsympathetically finish Vince off.

With her father lying bloodied and beaten on the canvas, Stephanie turns to give me a hug. And it's on.

We could see that this turn would give Vince a chance to get off TV every week. On camera, we played it out by having Vince so disgusted over losing his daughter that he leaves the company. Just walks away. Stephanie and I take full control of the family business and bring it into what we referred to as "The McMahon-Helmsley Era."

The story line was scorching. Not only was I the most sinister character on the show, but as one half of the brain trust, no one could stop me. I could do whatever I wanted. I won back the World title and it drove the fans insane. I was already one of the top guys before we started the story line of the McMahon-Helmsley Era, and it established me as unquestionably the top heel in the business. We brought some of the old DX guys back into the fold to give me a malicious gang willing to do whatever I needed them to.

We were attacking the Superstars the fans adored. We fired Mick Foley when we got tired of ripping him apart on a nightly basis and made life miserable for the People's Champ, The Rock. The hatred the fans had for us was like nothing I had ever seen. There were threats against me on a regular basis. Fans threw things at Steph pretty much every night in the ring.

"The McMahon-Helmsley Era" was a high point not only in my professional career but also in my personal life.

TRIPLE H

I love making life miserable for the People's Champ, The Rock.

I remember her getting nailed with a baseball one time. We had to stay in separate hotels to throw the fans off. It was totally out of control.

The professional in me was thrilled with how all of this was progressing. We had hit an emotional nerve with the fans and, as a result, had the most passionate, enthusiastic crowds you could imagine at events all over the country. I also had some amazing guys to work with in the ring.

During the time we were torturing him, Mick Foley and I put together several excellent matches that tore down the houses. Working with Mick is always a special experience, and these matches lived up to it for me. The Rock and I accomplished what most people thought was impossible—we competed in an Ironman match. That's wrestling for sixty straight minutes without taking a break. The physical and psychological toll this match puts on your body is indescribable. You need to have the stamina to perform for

an hour in a match with enough emotional turns to keep the fans engaged the entire time. You have to know when to give them the payoff they need . . . and when to take it away. If there was anybody I'd be able to pull this feat off with, it was The Rock. And we did.

Throw in a feud with Stone Cold Steve Austin and a couple of merciless beatings of other Superstars, and the McMahon-Helmsley Era had been going strong for well over a year with no signs of slowing down.

There was one twist where Steve Austin and I forged an unlikely alliance to capture the Tag Team Championship in April 2001. We were defending our titles against Chris Jericho and Chris Benoit one night on *Raw*. Live television.

We moved toward the end, into a sequence that was going to steamroll us to the finish. Chris Jericho had Austin in his finishing move—the Walls of Jericho—and I was supposed to jump in the ring and hit him from behind to get him to release the hold. I pretty much executed as planned, only the instant I planted my left leg on the canvas to come through with a shot to Jericho's neck, I felt a searing pain in my leg, like someone stabbed my thigh with a knife and ripped it down to the knee. The pain was intense. My leg filled with uncomfortable warmth. I could feel my quad muscle roll up my leg as I collapsed, unable to support myself.

My momentum carried me through to hit Chris, and he flew out of the ring. I was supposed to follow him out to the floor, but I knew I was hurt bad. I didn't have time to think about what to do. I just did what came naturally. I made my way out of the ring and over to Chris to finish the match. We were on live television, so it never truly dawned on me to do anything other than finish the match as planned, to push the pain out of my mind and give the fans what they deserved—the kind of match they paid to see.

When I got over to Chris, he could see something was wrong because I was hopping on one leg. I told him I was hurt real bad and he asked what I wanted to do, if I wanted to call an end to the match. "No, no. Let's just finish it."

"Are you sure?"

"Absolutely . . . let's do it."

The reason Chris was uneasy about continuing with what we planned was because he knew what was coming up next. We made our way over to the announcer's table and climbed on top to slug it out for a little bit. Eventually, Chris knocked me down and put me in the Walls of Jericho, a move that keeps you on your stomach while Chris stands over you, using your feet to stretch your legs back as far as they can go. This move forces your quads to support all of the pressure.

Before we were in this spot it hadn't dawned on me to do anything other than get the job done as planned. Once I was in the move, though, I was thinking, *You dumb jackass . . . what were you thinking with this?* If you watch the tape, you'll see that I wasn't in that move for more than thirty seconds, but at the time it felt like an hour to me. The pain was excruciating. The entire segment moved in slow motion; I couldn't believe time took as long as it did to melt away. My quad was completely torn at this point, and it felt like Chris was ripping my entire leg off with it.

The thirty seconds was over. Chris let go and raced back in the ring.

Next up for me was getting myself off the table, down to the floor. When I accomplished that, I hopped over to retrieve a sledgehammer I had hidden under the ring. I used the ropes to pull me up and inside. The pain was tormenting. I hopped over to where Benoit was now covering Austin and lunged to hit him with the hammer, only he moved at the last second, forcing me to hit Austin. Jericho walloped me from behind, knocking me out of the ring again as they covered Austin to notch the victory. I crashed down to the concrete floor, curled into the fetal position, and waited for the trainer.

"What's wrong? Where are you hurt?"

"I tore my quad."

"You didn't tear your quad. Trust me, you didn't do that."

The trainer didn't believe me at first because a full tear of the quad is just such an uncommon injury that he didn't expect to see it when he came out and he sure didn't think there was any way I could have finished wrestling the match with one. But I know my body. I felt it tear off.

The last memory I have from out on the floor that night is lying down in horrific pain already thinking about my return. All that's running through my head was *I wonder if I can be back for* SummerSlam. *That's in four months, so if I work hard I should be able to make it.* I had no idea of the actual extent of the injury I had suffered, yet I was already trying to calculate how long I'd be out with it.

I was in Birmingham, Alabama, early the next day to see Dr. James Andrews, perhaps the foremost orthopedic surgeon in the world. Dr. Andrews was going to let me know exactly how much damage I had suffered the night before and what my chances were to get back in the ring.

As you're about to find out, my background in bodybuilding is what fueled my ability to overcome this most challenging obstacle in my life. I can tell you all day that bodybuilding helps you learn self-discipline and how to set goals. But my ability to return from this injury is tangible proof that it's not bullshit.

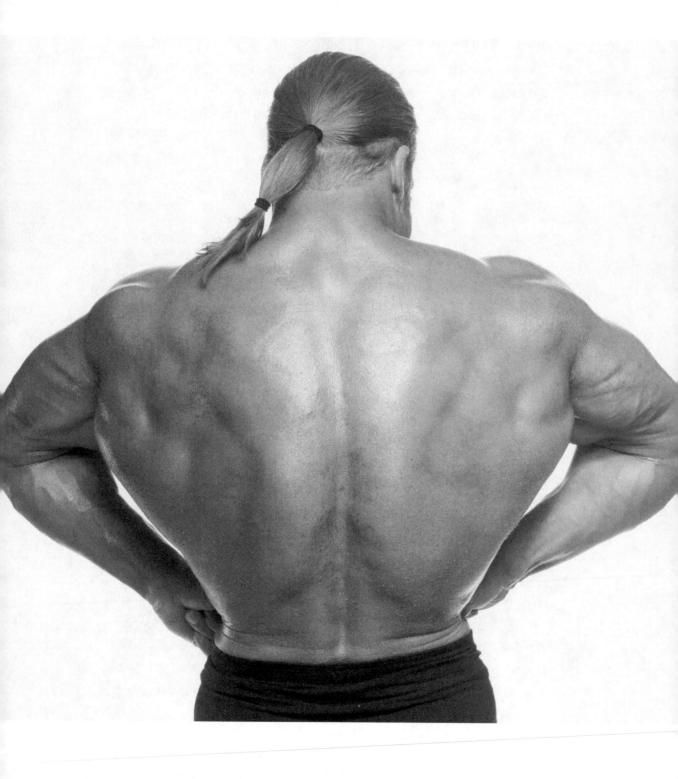

12. TRAINING THE BACK AND REAR DELTOIDS

I pair up these two muscle groups because, like the triceps do with the shoulders, the rear delts get a good pump as I do my back work.

Back Exercise #1: Wide-Grip Pulldown

You can do this exercise to either the front or the back to blast new muscle in your upper back and add width. Most bodybuilders prefer to go behind their head with it because you can feel the muscle working. There's also less of a tendency to lean back as you lower the bar—a technical error that turns this exercise into more of a rowing motion and not nearly as effective.

Back Exercise #2: Barbell Bent-Over Row

This is a hard-core exercise that will build mass and thickness to your upper back. Although the lower back isn't the primary focus of this one, it will also benefit from it.

Back Exercise #3: Dumbbell Row

Another exercise that really works your upper back. The difference between the Barbell and Dumbbell Rows is that by working each arm independently of the other, the dumbbells allow for better muscle contraction. If I'm more in the mood for cable work, I do seated cable rows instead of using the dumbbells. It has the same effect on your muscles.

Back Exercise #4: Close-Grip Pulldown

The way I usually like to work my back is to start with exercises that focus on my upper back and then work my way down. With the first three out of the way, I'm now moving on down. I use the V-grip handle for this exercise and pull to the front to tie in lower in the lats. I stay very strict, pulling the bar down to my lower chest and contracting the lower part of my back with every rep.

Back Exercise #5: Hyperextension

Hyperextensions are a great way to chisel the spinal erectors in your back. Most days, I do only 1 set of them for 15 reps.

I work a set of hyperextensions to develop the spinal erectors in my lower back.

Back Exercise #6: Partial Deadlift

I'm not a fan of full deadlifts because the bottom part of the exercise is all hip and ass and since I'm not Jennifer Lopez, I'm not looking to build up a gigantic ass. I prefer the three-quarter deadlift. It's the same form as a regular deadlift, only I come down to the top of my shin. Once I bring the bar back up, I try to roll my shoulders to contract my lats and lower back.

REAR DELTOIDS EXERCISES

Rear Delts Exercise #1: Rear-Delt Fly

Do 2 or 3 sets of rear-delt flys to get warmed up for the final exercise of this session. Working on your rear delts using the fly machine targets the muscle and allows you to crush the rear delts at the end of the long back session.

Rear Delts Exercise #2: Bent-Over Dumbbell Raise

A great way to end your training day. Get back to normal routine— 1 warm-up set, 3 working sets—for this exercise. When executed with precision, the rear-delt bent-over dumbbell raises will burn this hard-to-train muscle to a crisp and have you feeling great as you walk out of the gym for the day.

For detailed instructions on the exercises in this chapter, see color pages 20–27.

Dr. Andrews didn't have to look at the MRI to know right off that I tore my quad. He knew by touching my leg and hearing me describe what happened. The medical explanation was a tear of the vastus intermedius—the largest part of the quadriceps muscle group and one of the largest muscles of the entire body.

13. THE LONG JOURNEY BACK

After that first meeting, Dr. Andrews said he believed I'd be out for about six months. When they went in to do the surgery, though, it turned out to be a much worse tear than they originally thought and they told me I should prepare to be out for up to one year. This actually turned out to be a case where the doctor held back a little because he didn't want to obliterate any positive feelings about getting better.

Dr. Andrews explained to me a few months later that as he walked out of surgery that day, he doubted that I'd ever make it back. Coming back in a year would be amazing; he expected my professional wrestling career was over.

Hearing all this from him for the first time, realizing how close I was to having my career finished, was an emotional thing. You never think about getting hurt when you're out there. I certainly didn't because I'd been lucky up to that point, avoiding serious injury throughout my career. Now here I was in Birmingham having someone tell me that it could all be over. One instant inside the ring could end my entire career just like that. Done.

A sports magazine called Dr. Andrews toward the end of my rehab, asking him to contribute to an article on quad tears. They wanted him to talk about athletes he treated who came back after receiving a full quad repair. He told them he'd be happy to contribute, just give him a couple of days to

Despite successful surgery on my torn quadriceps muscle, I would never have wrestled again without the help of my physical therapist, Kevin Wilk.

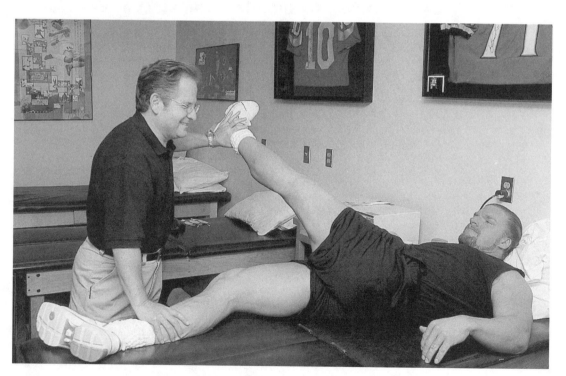

go over his notes and call some other doctors for information. Well, he went through his files, made a bunch of phone calls, and he couldn't find any.

Every doctor he called, every sports team he reached out to, he couldn't find one person. On the day he finally gave up looking, he came over to me to tell me the story and said, "You're gonna be my first guy on this, so don't screw up! You're an example." Even though he was kidding around with me, his message hit me hard. I didn't realize nobody had ever come back from this thing. I knew it was something that was difficult to come back from, but possible. You know one of those injuries where the doctor would say something like, "This is a tough rehab, but a few guys have come back from it and you can be one of them if you work real hard at it." It may sound stupid now, but at the time, that's what I thought they meant by "career-ending." I didn't realize they meant that *no one* had really ever done this before. And especially with an impact sport like professional wrestling. It's not like I was going out there to play golf—I was going to be pushing my body to the limit every night.

During one of Dr. Andrews's first visits after the surgery, we started talking about my rehab in the immediate future.

"Kevin (Wilk) is the best rehab guy in the world, so—"

"Great, I'll stay here, then," I said before he could go any further.

"Stay here? What do you mean? The whole time?"

"Yeah. I'll just stay here, in Birmingham, for as long as I need. Is that an option—can I do all my rehab here?"

"Yes, if you'd like to."

The only thing I cared about was getting back in that ring, even if it meant moving to Birmingham for ten months.

The rehab facility Dr. Andrews has down there is just incredible. Everything about it is top-notch. Dr. Andrews would be the first person to tell you that he puts you back together, but the rehab facility is what gets you back to doing what you do. The guy there who is just as responsible for the incredible success of the practice, but doesn't get mentioned as much as Dr. Andrews, is Kevin Wilk, one of the top physical therapists in the world. I give him just as much credit as I do Dr. Andrews for getting me back in the ring. I couldn't have done it without his support; he was behind me one hundred percent.

It didn't matter what I wanted to do. If I wanted to be there twenty-four hours a day, he would have found a way for me to be there. As long as I wasn't hurting myself, he let me go.

When it came time for it, Vince sent a ring down to Birmingham and they made some space for it in the building across the street. They wanted to watch me in the ring so they could see what movements I needed to strengthen. When I hit the ropes, when I bumped, they could see exactly what areas of my leg I needed to build. When I took my first couple of bumps, they could see that I was slow getting up, so they tried to figure out how they could strengthen the part of my leg that would let me push up off the mat quicker.

Through all of this, one of the things that allowed me to overcome every challenge was my background in bodybuilding. It was never a question for me of worrying about it all. I never thought, *How am I going to endure all of this? Get the surgery, go home, find a rehab place, learn to walk again—it's all too much.* I just took it one step at a time and knew I had to get through each part to eventually arrive where I wanted to go. It was all about setting goals—something I learned years earlier as a teenage bodybuilder. If I looked at the monumental task of the entire thing as just

Maintaining a positive attitude throughout my rehab kept me focused on returning to the ring.

one big event I might have lost it. If I thought *I'm gonna be out a whole year with this!* I might not have made it because I would have been focused only on the ending and wouldn't have drawn any encouragement from the progress I was making along the way. It's that progress that kept me motivated, that kept me coming back every morning.

One of the first things I did was make a list of general goals to cover the early part of my rehab:

- **Get the epidural out of my back**

- **Get out of the hospital**

- **Wiggle my foot**

- **Get out of the wheelchair and up on crutches**

- **Get rid of one crutch**

- **Walk with just a brace**

- **Walk without the help of a brace**

- **Walk without a limp**

As I achieved all of these goals, the only thing on my mind every morning when I walked into rehab was how much I was going to increase the range of motion of my leg. One of the hardest thresholds to cross with this exercise is moving your leg far enough to break up the scar tissue. It puts you in an excruciating amount of pain.

There were a few ways they would work on increasing my range at the rehab facility. The first was a manual method where I would lie down on a table and they would push on my leg until I felt it just couldn't go anymore. Once I got a little bit of the motion back, they gave me an apparatus to wear on my leg while I slept. It would move my leg ever so slightly throughout the night, to ensure it didn't stiffen up and set me back.

The range of motion got measured daily and the degree of change from day to day was so minor that it looked exactly the same. I knew from basic bodybuilding that small, realistic goals are the way to go. So I'd wake up with a positive attitude every morning, ready to take a small step forward on my giant journey to long-term recovery.

If my range was 15 the day before, I wanted 16 before I walked out of there the next day. No matter what, I wasn't leaving until I got my 16. When I

Increasing my leg's range of motion every day was an excruciating goal I had set for myself.

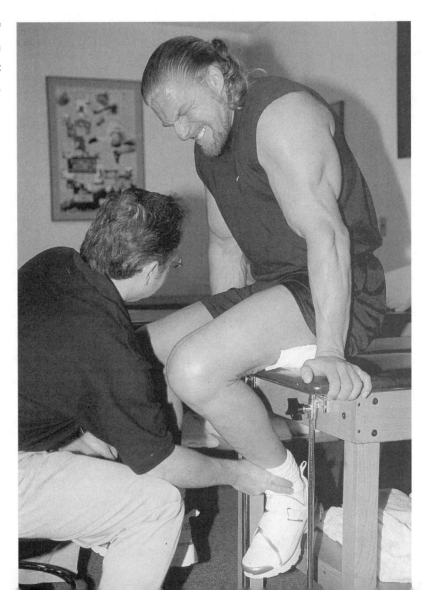

was fully recovered, Kevin and some of the other guys told me there were a few days where they were finally like, "Great! All right . . . you got your number," even though I didn't. That was the only way they could get me out of there some nights and keep me positive.

The self-discipline and work ethic I picked up from bodybuilding is what kept me coming back every morning to strive for that number on the range. It taught me how to push myself, mentally and physically, past the usual limits of strength and endurance. My history with bodybuilding served as an internal alarm clock that kicked my ass out of bed every morning. I kept pretty much the same exact schedule for the nine months I was in Alabama.

- **Get to rehab at 9 A.M. and stay there until 6 P.M.**

- **Go back to the hotel for a protein shake**

- **Have the hotel shuttle bus driver drop me off at the gym down the road**

- **Stay there until around 9 P.M.**

- **Go back to the hotel**

- **Eat dinner**

- **Talk on the phone or watch TV**

- **Go to sleep**

This is what I did for nine months straight. I refused to let up. The only time I wasn't at the rehab facility during the days were the times I'd leave for an hour to have lunch with Kevin. Even when I was on crutches or in the wheelchair, I'd go over to the gym and do whatever I could.

On the weekends, I wasn't scheduled to be at the rehab facility, but I was there every Saturday and Sunday for nine months. Weekdays I did double sessions, with the facility and the gym. I took it easy on the weekends, only going to rehab, taking the nights off.

I don't see this story like I'm bragging. Pushing my body to the limit to get back to wrestling was never something I contemplated. I certainly never thought I was doing anything heroic or going through this big deal that other people wouldn't do. All I knew was that I had to work my ass off to get back to the thing I loved. Like finishing the match that put me in this situation, giving one hundred percent to my rehab was the only thing I considered.

But I know that not every athlete shares this passion. While I was down there, I'd watch NFL guys come in and out, half-assing their workouts, or just not show up in the afternoon, and that infuriated me. There was this other guy down there, someone named one of the NBA's fifty greatest players a few years ago, who really pissed me off. I saw him in there one day and they couldn't get him to stop reading the newspaper and get on the table for treatment. They practically had to beg him. Here's a guy making millions of dollars to play a game and he can't even be bothered to stop reading the newspaper. I never understood that attitude.

I don't give a shit if I had the biggest year of all time or won $500 million in the lottery and never had to work again, I'd still do this. I just love it. And that was the thing about rehab to me. It never seemed like I was making a sacrifice. I saw it as, *Holy shit, I may not be able to wrestle anymore so*

I gotta do whatever I gotta do because I'm not ready to give that up yet. I knew I wasn't done yet. There were so many things I wanted to accomplish in the business yet and I had to figure out a way back. In my mind, that's all I did. And I didn't do it alone.

Dr. Andrews, Kevin Wilk, and their entire team down there in Birmingham, who I can't possibly say enough about, worked and supported me through nine months of intense rehab. I had my family and friends with me through the entire ordeal. The most important person to me through the entire process, though, was Steph. I'll get into our relationship later, but by this time, life had imitated art, as we were truly in love.

Years of dedicated weight training taught me to take my rehab one day at a time.

My injury couldn't have happened at a worse time as it related to our developing romance. We had just started to get serious, and then the next thing I knew I was moving down to Birmingham, away from her, for almost a year. But she stayed with me through the entire ordeal. She slept in my hospital room when I was recovering from surgery, making sure I had anything I needed. She was down in Birmingham every chance she had, cheering me on in rehab, setting up her computer on the patient

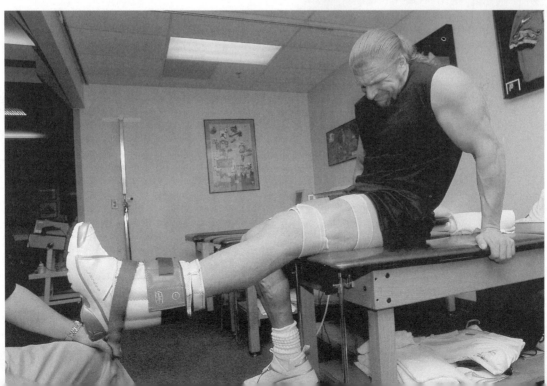

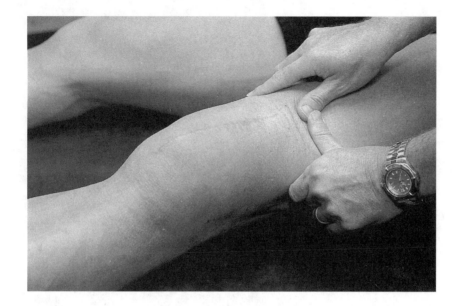

It's a battle scar I could have done without, but I'm just glad my leg works better than ever.

tables to check e-mail and conduct business. She was an incredible source of support and inspiration for me.

And at the end of 2001, I was ready to make my return.

For the weeks leading up to it, the build that the company gave me was unbelievable from the standpoint of making people anticipate my return. As we got closer and closer to the actual day—January 7, 2002, a live *Raw* from Madison Square Garden—-the television work the company put together promoting my return had the fans ready.

I had done a couple of house shows the weekend prior to the Garden, partly because I needed to get in some live match work, but also because I didn't want to freak out when I got to MSG. That weekend we did unbelievable business at the house shows because of how well they advertised I'd be there. We sold out the buildings at a time when we weren't really doing any sellouts. We set an all-time record in Springfield for the building and for us. So over the weekend, I started to feel confident that my return was going to be good, but that day at the Garden—and this is something that Austin and I talked about when he came back from his neck surgery— somewhere in the back of your mind you're thinking, *What if they don't care? What if when I walk through that curtain they all say, "Oh, you're back? Big deal."* You can't help but wonder about it.

Right up until my music hit I was shitting my pants. I remember standing just behind the curtain, where all the TV monitors are, when the graphic came up on the screen.

UP NEXT: THE GAME MAKES HIS RETURN!

When I saw that, I thought, *Oh God, here we go.* It became real at that moment. There was nothing standing in my way. The crowd had been buzzing all night, breaking out into random chants of "Triple H . . . Triple H . . . Triple H!" but once this graphic hit and they knew it was minutes away, the chanting didn't stop. It's funny, even at this point I still doubted that they would care. I mean, listening to a packed MSG cheering my name, trembling at the thought of my busting through the curtains any second, how could I not think that it was going to be a great night? I don't know.

When my music hit, the building absolutely exploded. I gave Vince a look that if it could talk, would have said, "Holy shit! I can't believe this!" The volume doubled when I walked out. It blew my mind.

I was so jazzed up through the whole performance. The atmosphere out there was electric. I couldn't have been any higher emotionally. To be at Madison Square Garden—the most famous arena in the world— getting this type of reaction was absolutely mind-boggling to me. It was

I'll always be grateful
to the MSG fans who
welcomed me back to
Raw on January 7, 2002.

DAY ONE (HEAVY DAY)—CHEST, SHOULDERS, TRICEPS

Front Military Dumbbell Presses

Sit in a chair with high back support. Rest your feet flat on the floor, directly in front of you, with your toes pointing straight ahead. With palms facing out, hold two dumbbells so your arms are locked in a 90-degree angle. Slowly raise the dumbbells up until your arms straighten out. Lower them back to the starting position.

1

Lateral Raises

Stand with your feet shoulder-width apart and your shoulders slightly hunched forward. Grab two dumbbells with your palms facing your body. Hold the dumbbells about ten inches apart. Raise the dumbbells up and out, rotating your palms to face the floor, until the dumbbells are about even with your shoulders. Lower them back down to the starting position. Make sure your motions are slow, so you are not swinging the dumbbells up and down uncontrollably.

Dumbbell Front Raises

Stand with your feet shoulder-width apart. With your palms facing toward you, have the dumbbells up against the front of your thighs. One arm at a time, raise the dumbbell straight in front of you until your arm is fully extended. Slowly lower it back down to the starting position and repeat the motion with the other arm.

Dumbbell Shrugs

Stand with your legs shoulder-width apart, with dumbbells down at your sides. Raise your shoulders up as high as they can go—try to touch your ears with them. When your shoulders are at their apex, hold them there for a long count. Lower them back down to the starting position.

Overhead Rope Extensions

Stand with your back facing a rope attached to the high pulley. Take hold of it with your palms facing each other. Bend at the waist and pull the rope forward until your arms are locked at a 90-degree angle. This is the starting position. Pull the rope forward until your arms are fully extended. Return to the starting position.

Triceps Pushdowns

Stand with your feet a little wider than shoulder-width apart. Take hold of the rope attachment with your palms facing inward. Pull your elbows in as close to your body as you can. Pull the rope down until your arms are fully extended or as far as you can go. Slowly return to the starting position.

Lying Triceps Extensions (Skull Crushers)

Lie on a flat bench with your feet flat on the floor and your head resting high up on the bench. Hold an **E-Z Curl** bar, with your hands about six inches apart, straight up over your chest. Bend at the elbows and slowly lower the bar until it is only inches from your fore-head. Raise the bar back up to the starting position.

11

Dumbbell French Presses

Take a seat on a weight bench with no back support. Make sure your feet are flat on the floor, pointing straight ahead. Pick up a dumbbell and hold it straight up over the back of your head. Slowly lower it down as far as you can go. You should feel a deep stretch in your triceps. Raise the dumbbell back up to the starting position.

DAY TWO (LIGHT DAY)—BACK, BICEPS, LEGS

Riding the Bike

Before you start your leg routine, jump on the exercise bike to increase your heart rate and get your legs warmed up for what they're about to go through.

Leg Extensions

Take a seat on the leg extension machine. You can use either the one that works both legs at once or each independently. Use the handgrips to make certain you remain firmly planted in the seat. Hook your legs under the pads. The pads should rest at the very bottom of your shin. Extend your legs out until they are straight or as far as they can go. Come back to the starting position.

Leg Presses

Take your position on the leg press machine. Put both feet on the plate, keeping them about shoulder-width apart. Take hold of the handgrips on the side to help keep you in place. Your legs should not be one-hundred-percent extended when in the "up" position. When set, slowly bring the weight down toward your body until your legs form a 90-degree angle. Return the plate to the starting position.

Machine Squats

Rest the bar on your shoulders and stand with your feet slightly more than shoulder-width apart. Your hands should be on the bar, about one foot away from your shoulders. Slowly dip your body down as you keep your back as straight as you can. Try to get your back down far enough so your legs are forming a 90-degree angle. Rise back up to the starting position.

Lying Leg Curls

Take your position on the lying leg curl machine. The pad should sit about halfway between your knee and your calf. Pull your ankle up toward you as far as you can. Slowly return it to the starting position. Try not to move your back or shoulders while performing this exercise. Focus on the hamstrings doing all your work.

Seated Calf Raises

Take a seat on the seated calf machine. Hook your thighs under the pad and rest the balls of your feet on the bar below. Sit up straight and take hold of the handgrips. Drop your heels down toward the ground, and then push up with the balls of your feet so you can feel your calves fully contracted. Slowly return your heels back toward the ground.

DAY THREE (LIGHT DAY)— CHEST, SHOULDERS, TRICEPS

Wide-Grip Pulldowns

Attach a long bar with wide grips to the high pulley. Take a seat and tuck your thighs under the pads to help keep you firmly planted. Have your feet flat on the floor. Grab hold of the bar and slowly pull it down in front of you. Continue down until the bar is as far as you can get it without sliding your head or back to an angle. Keep them both upright. With total control, return the bar to the starting position.

Close-Grip Pulldowns

Attach a close-grip extension to the high pulley.
Take a seat and tuck your thighs under the pads
to help keep you firmly planted. Have your feet
flat on the floor. Grab hold of the extension and
slowly pull it down in front of you. Bring it down
and try to touch your chest with it. Slide your
head and back as needed to pull the extension
all the way down to your chest. Slowly return to
the starting position.

Barbell Bent-Over Rows

Stand with your feet about ten inches apart. Slightly bend your knees. Bend at the waist to pick up the barbell. Keep your back straight and your head up so you are looking in front of you. Lift the barbell up to your lower abdomen. Focus on using the muscles in your back, not your arms, for this lift. Lower the bar back to the starting position.

Dumbbell Rows

You need a flat bench to help support you in this exercise. Pick up a dumbbell in your left hand. Place your right arm and right knee on the flat bench so your upper body is parallel to the floor. Keep your back straight and your weight forward. Your head should be up so you are looking in front of you. Let the dumbbell hang at an arm's length. Keep your elbow back as you lift the dumbbell straight up to your chest. Focus on using your upper back muscles, not your arms, to lift the dumbbell.

Bent-Over Long Bar Rows

Straddle one end of a barbell. Bend at the waist. Slightly bend your knees. Your back should be straight, but at about a 45-degree angle to the floor. Keep your head straight so you are looking in front of you. Place your hands on the inside of the plates. Raise the bar up to your body. Let it back down to an arm's length. Concentrate on working your back here, not lifting the barbell up with your arms.

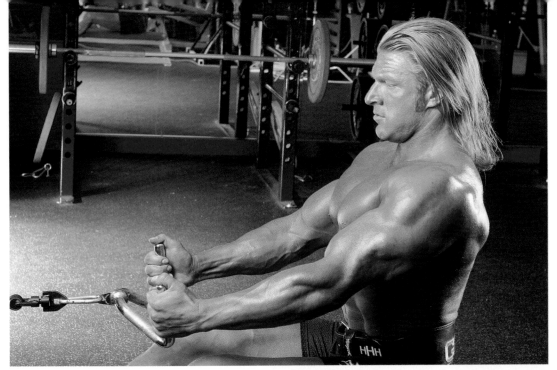

Seated Cable Rows

Take a seat at the low pulley cable rowing machine and make sure to have a close-grip attachment hooked in. Rest your feet flat against the footrests in front of you. Slightly bend your knees. Keep your back straight up. Hold your shoulders back. Start with the attachment at an arm's length and slowly pull it toward your body. Be sure not to rock your upper body for momentum. Use the muscles in your back, not your biceps, to pull the weights.

Hyperextensions

Lie facedown on a hyperextension board with your heels dug under the foot support down at the bottom. Cross your arms in front of you and pull them into your chest. Bend forward as far you can go. You will feel a deep stretch through your whole back, although it should be strongest in your lower-to-mid back.

Bent-Over Dumbbell Raises

Stand with your feet about ten inches apart, with your knees bent slightly. Bend at the waist. Your back should be parallel to the floor. Let the dumbbells hang down in front of you, with your palms facing in and your elbows slightly bent. Raise the dumbbells up and out to your side until they reach slightly lower than shoulder height. Your elbows should always be higher than your wrists. Return to the starting position.

DAY FOUR (HEAVY DAY)—
BACK, BICEPS, LEGS

Flat-Bench Barbell Press

Lie on a flat bench with your feet flat on the floor out to the sides. You should take a wide grip on the barbell, about one foot outside each shoulder. Slowly lower the bar until it grazes your chest. It should hit your upper chest, approximately six to eight inches below your chin. Return to the starting position.

Flat-Bench Dumbbell Presses

Lie on a flat bench. Your feet should be flat on the floor and out to the sides to help you remain balanced. Grab two dumbbells with your palms facing away from your body. Fully extend your arms straight up. The back of the dumbbell should be turned in. Slowly allow the weights to come down so each of your arms forms a 90-degree angle. Return to the starting position.

Incline-Bench Dumbbell Presses

Lie on an incline bench set so you're resting at about a 45-degree angle to the floor. Your feet should be flat on the floor and out to the sides to help you remain balanced. Grab two dumbbells with your palms facing away from your body. Fully extend your arms straight up. The back of the dumbbell should be turned in. Slowly allow the weights to come down so each of your arms forms a 90-degree angle. Return to the starting position.

Incline-Bench Dumbbell Flys

Lie on an incline bench set so you're resting at about a 45-degree angle to the floor. Your feet should be flat on the floor and out to the sides to help you remain balanced. Grab two dumbbells with your palms facing in and hold them up over your head in a way that angles the back of the dumbbell in. Slowly lower them down to the sides in a circular motion. Keep your wrists locked, but bend your elbows as needed. Push yourself until you feel a deep stretch across your entire chest. Return to the starting position.

Flat-Bench Dumbbell Flys

Lie on a flat bench with your head resting as high on the bench as it can be without hanging over it at all. Your feet should be flat on the floor and out to the sides to help you remain balanced. Grab two dumbbells with your palms facing in and hold them straight up. Slowly lower them down to the sides in a circular motion. Keep your wrists locked, but bend your elbows as needed. Push yourself until you feel a deep stretch across your entire chest. Return to the starting position.

Standing Cable Crossovers

Stand in the middle of two overhead pulleys. Your feet should be shoulder-width apart. Take hold of the attachments with your palms facing in. Stand up straight and keep your eyes looking ahead. Pull the attachments toward one another, almost as if you are trying to touch your palms together. Focus on contracting your pecs with each movement so the exercise targets those muscles, not your biceps.

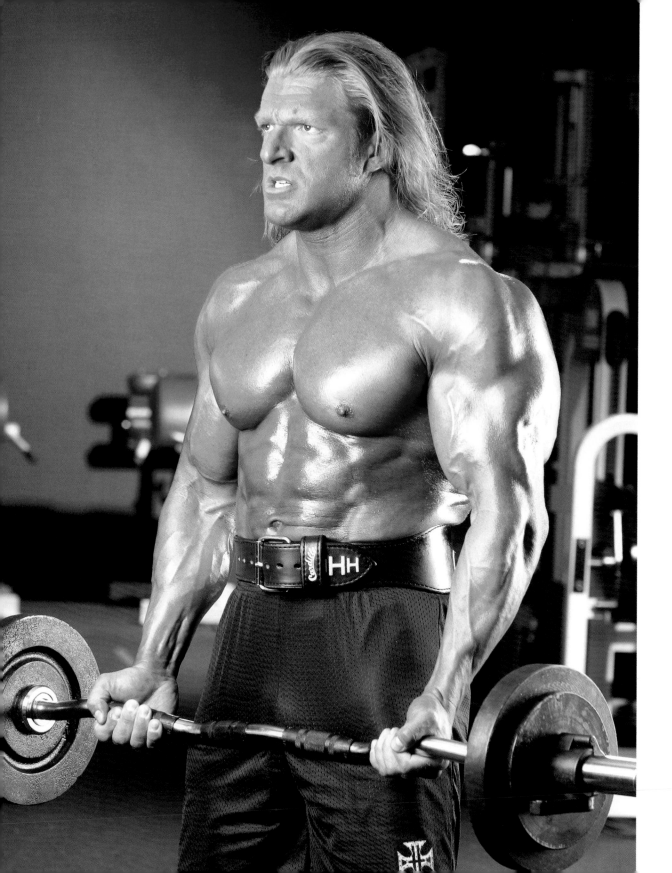

Barbell Curls

Stand with your feet shoulder-width apart and your toes pointing straight in front of you.
Take hold of an **E-Z Curl** barbell with your hands at slightly more than shoulder-width apart
and your palms facing outward. Pull the bar up to your chest. Keep your back straight as
you work on this one. Focus on using your biceps and do not rock your upper body back
and forth to gain momentum.

Seated Dumbbell Concentration Curls

Take a seat on a flat bench. Keep your legs flat on the floor, but spread your legs out. Take a dumbbell in your right hand and place your left hand on your left thigh for support. Turn your upper body away from the side you will be working. Let your working arm hang straight down. Lift the dumbbell up, using the elbow on the arm you're working on as a pivot point. Focus on the biceps getting all the work here. Return to the starting position. Repeat with the other arm.

One-Arm Dumbbell Preacher Curls

Take a seat at a preacher curl station and turn your body to one side. With the arm that is in front, take hold of a dumbbell. Place your other hand on top of the padding to help support you. Let your working arm hang straight down. Lift the dumbbell up toward your shoulder as high as you can. Visualize the biceps muscle contracting on every rep.

41

Alternating Seated Dumbbell Curls

Take a seat on an incline bench. Set it so you are only slightly reclining. Grab a dumbbell with one hand and your palm facing out. Let that working arm hang down at your side. Lift the dumbbell up toward your shoulder as high as you can. Make sure to keep your lower back flat against the seat during the entire motion. Your shoulders should be hunched forward a bit. Return to the starting position. Complete the exercise with the other arm.

Overhead Cable Curls

Stand in the middle of two overhead pulleys. Your feet should be shoulder-width apart. Take hold of the attachments with your palms facing away from your body. Your starting position should have your arms forming about a 135-degree angle. Pull the attachments toward your head, turning your wrists inward as you do. Keep your back as straight as you can the whole time. Slowly return to the starting position.

ABS

Stairmaster

The Stairmaster provides a great cardio workout to get your body warmed up before start-ing any abs exercises. Cardio is the best way to burn the fat covering your abs, which will help you get that "six-pack" look.

Flat-Bench Leg Raises

Take a seat on the end of a flat bench. Extend your legs out in front of you so your heels are touching the ground. Lean back so your back creates about a 45-degree angle with the bench. Grab hold of the bench right under your back. Slowly lift your legs up off the ground as far as you can. Return them to the starting position.

Cross-Body Crunches

Lie on your back with your heels flat on the floor about 18 inches in front of you. Put your hands behind your head. Raise your head off the floor and reach your right elbow across your body as if you want to touch your left knee with it. Lower your back to the starting position and repeat the move with your left elbow. As you move up and down, focus on contracting your abs each time.

Crunches

Lie on your back with your heels flat on the floor about 18 inches in front of you. Cross your arms and rest them high up on your chest. Raise your head off the floor as far as you can. Keep your lower back flat on the floor. Slowly lower your back to the starting position. As you move up and down, focus on contracting your abs each time.

Crunches with Raised Legs

Lie on your back with your legs raised so they are at a 90-degree angle. Fold your arms behind your head and grasp them together at the palms. Raise your head off the floor toward your legs as far as you can. Keep your lower back flat on the floor. Slowly lower your back to the starting position. As you move up and down, focus on contracting your abs each time.

such an amazing rush that I almost couldn't hold it together out there in the ring.

When I got back through the curtain and made sure I was out of sight, I lost it. I was bawling. Certainly not out of sadness. It was an appreciation. The whole ordeal was just so emotional for me—what I'd gone through, what I almost lost, the appreciation the fans showed me—it all just hit me at once and I lost it.

If I had busted my ass for ten months and everything I had gone through with my leg was just for that one moment, that one moment when I walked through that curtain and heard that crowd and it all shut off right there, it would have all been worth it. Just for that moment. That's how much it meant to me.

To this day, fans still come up to me to tell me they were there that night and usually say something like, "I've never experienced anything like that in my life."

And neither have I.

Thank you all for that.

Legs are always a critical exercise day for me due to the injury.

I don't train my legs to achieve sheer size. My legs are functional for what I need to accomplish as a professional wrestler. Remember, you need to mold your exercise regimen to meet your personal goals.

14. TRAINING YOUR LEGS

I work to blend mass, speed, endurance, agility, and flexibility with my leg training. To do this, my routine emphasizes a lower-weight, higher-rep approach.

The legs are actually a unique muscle because they can achieve both strength and endurance in a way no other muscle can. If you built them up, you could move 500 pounds with your legs or you could run for an hour. But would you be able to bench-press for an hour straight? Didn't think so.

Your legs can go beyond what you think are their limits. Most times when you're training your legs and think you've reached failure, you can actually keep going. It's just the way your legs were built—so they could walk for miles and miles on end.

I start off all my leg days by riding the bike for ten minutes to get my heart rate up to about eighty-five percent of its target zone.

LEG EXTENSION EXERCISES

Leg Exercise #1: Leg Extension

Leg extensions do two things for me. They train the quadriceps as thoroughly as possible while warming up the entire muscle for the serious training session I'm about to have.

I'll do 4 sets to failure, then finish up by running the rack.

Leg Exercise #2: Leg Press

The emphasis here is to add significant size to the quadriceps muscle. I'll go with the usual 4 sets, all to failure, but I try to get between 15 and 20 reps on each set.

Since my quad injury, I concentrate on lower weights and higher reps during leg exercises.

Leg Exercise #3: Hack Squat

You could substitute walking lunges here if you'd like. Regardless of which one I'm doing, I go for 2–3 sets of 15–20 reps to finish the quad session.

Leg Exercise #4: Lying Leg Curl

Now I'm looking to hit the hamstrings, and this machine is a great way to do it. You can feel the burn in your hamstring, letting you know this one is working.

Leg Exercise #5: Stiff-legged Deadlift

Standing leg curls are a great alternative here as well. Either way, pump out 3 sets of 15–20 reps.

CALF EXERCISES

Calf Exercise #1: Standing Calf Raise

This is an old-fashioned calf exercise to build up the overall size of your calves.

Calf Exercise #2: Seated Calf Raise

This variation of the calf raise focuses more on defining the lower and outer areas of your calf muscles.

For detailed instructions on the exercises in this chapter, see color pages 14–19.

Once I got settled in again after the injury, it became clear that my character wasn't going to lose any steam with the fans. It was a bit different now than before the injury, because instead of being a full-fledged heel, I was sort of in between. I was the guy you cheered for

but didn't quite trust. I had been such a prick for the last few years that the fans weren't buying into this new attitude. They were waiting for me to commit some horrendous act and then they'd say, "See, we knew he wasn't a good guy!"

But it didn't happen right away. Regardless of whether they thought I was good or bad or somewhere in between, they felt something for me. There was an obvious connection between me and the fans, and that's all that matters in this business. Within a few months, I was the World Champion again. I won the title in 2002 at *WrestleMania X8*. Things were going great, not only for me but for the company as a whole.

Then a curious decision was made. Because of one night in Montreal, Canada, where Hulk Hogan was cheered like a god, the office decided to take the title off me and put it on him. This was a decision pushed by certain people inside the business. Not to sound bitter about the whole ordeal, but it was led by people who believed that the only reason I was in the spot in the first place was because of my personal relationship with Steph. So these people, who were against my being champion, convinced some others that we needed to go in a different direction. There were a few people who were fighting it, who knew it was the worst thing we could have done. As for me, there wasn't much I could say.

The fact is that my return sparked business. I'm not being arrogant, but these are the facts. At the time the decision was made, house show numbers were up since my return, TV ratings were up since my return, everything was up since I returned. And that all reversed when they switched the title over to Hogan. The only way to come out of it was to turn me back into a heel and let me get back to doing what I was best at.

When I dropped the title to Hogan and shook his hand and all that, the fans didn't buy it. They didn't buy my character acting like that, they didn't buy Hogan beating me, they didn't buy a lot of it. And ratings went down.

It wasn't a great situation all around. It didn't help my character; it ended my babyface run before it really got started. And worst of all, it was bad for the company.

It was just meant for me to go back to being a heel, which I prefer anyway, so I didn't really mind. It's been a couple of years now, and I still haven't really gotten another chance at being a babyface. And I may never. It doesn't bother me, though. I know another guy who has gone his whole career without getting in one solid, long-term run as a babyface—Ric Flair.

■　　　■　　　■

When I was a kid watching pro wrestling and started to have thoughts about doing it for a living, the only guy I ever wanted to be was Ric Flair. I always thought he was awesome.

When I would watch wrestling with my dad, I loved Flair and my dad hated him. Ric had a habit of getting beat up all the time, but finding a way to hold on to the title. This made my dad think he was a terrible wrestler. What stuck out for me, though, was that whenever he wrestled somebody, that person had a better match than they ever had in the past. And the way he could work the entire crowd into a frenzy, dying to see him get his ass kicked. The reaction he was getting was because his opponent was beating the shit out of him, but Ric was really the one orchestrating the entire thing. I just thought everything about him was awesome.

When Ric joined WWE in 2002, I was excited to have him, but when he came in he was very down on himself. He was insecure and self-conscious about his work. He wasn't the Ric Flair that I had known in WCW or heard stories about over the years. It was all a tribute to how big of a moron Eric Bischoff was in the business. He took people who love this business more than anything—guys like Ric and Arn—and made them absolutely hate it. Guys who should have been lifers in the business found themselves despising it. It was truly amazing.

Ric was nice and cordial to everyone, but he kept to himself for the most part. I knew him back in my days with WCW, so I was friendly with him when he got here. The more time I spent with him, the more I realized he needed to be propped back up a little bit. So I started to spend even more time with him, talking to him about whatever he wanted to talk about. I found myself helping Ric if he needed it, and because of this we became close friends.

As he started to get back into the swing of things, and trusted me to the point where he was sharing a lot of thoughts about the business, I came to see that we weren't using Ric to his full potential on the show. We were

It's been a privilege and an honor to work with Ric.

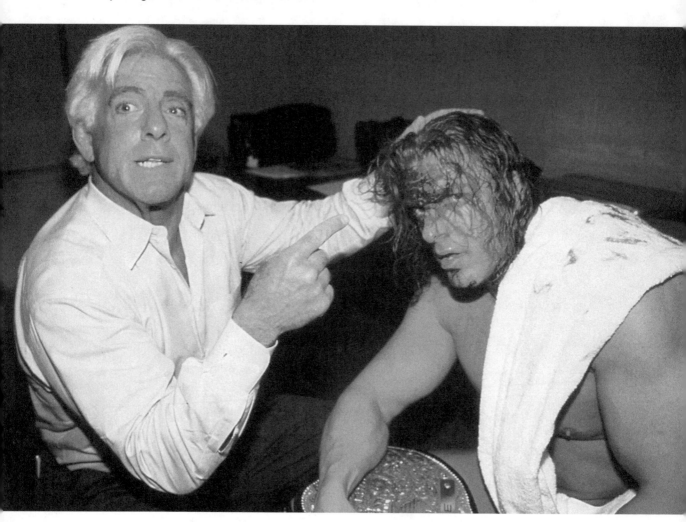

using him as a babyface in a limited role, and I knew he had much more to offer. He even admitted to me that he wanted to start wrestling a little bit more.

An idea that had been working its way through me at the time was starting another faction. Sort of like a DX, but one that would be heels through and through. I knew the company needed to build new talent, and I felt that much like Shawn did with DX, we could take a group of young guys and let them get a rub off established stars. I first talked to Vince and Steph about it, and they were cool with the idea. Then I talked to Ric because I knew he would be an important factor in the group for so many reasons. He could give a rub, as a heel, to all these different guys we brought in with us. Plus, when you're doing a group angle and you're together all the time, talking to one another at the building all day, you're going to learn from one another. I knew that any younger guys we brought in would benefit immeasurably from being around Ric all the time. And for Ric, having all these guys with him meant he could wrestle more. It wouldn't hurt his opponent to lose to a fifty-four-year-old who had a gang of pricks helping him out, but it would hurt a guy's credibility to lose one-on-one to a fifty-four-year-old if it wasn't done right.

Ric was interested in the idea, so we started looking at different guys to figure out who we were going to include in this group. We looked at everyone who was in the company at the time. He and I scouted each guy, watching them every night, examining their every move, studying them as we decided who we wanted to do this with. We chose the two guys we thought could do it: Randy Orton and Dave Batista.

Our picks were based on so much more than just how they did in the ring. What drew Arn and those guys to me that day in the WCW locker room

TRIPLE H

was that they could see my passion for the business. They knew I was one of them. Ric and I needed that attitude in whoever we chose to join us. We needed guys who would give their all. Guys who would listen when we tried to teach them something. Guys who would ask a lot of questions. Who really wanted it. Both Randy and Dave had all of that.

Once we got the group up and running, the dynamic between Ric and me was great. I mean, we got along right from the get-go as far as our personalities went. He and I share a lot of the same philosophies about the business and a lot of things outside the business. There were no struggles there.

The struggle for me was getting Ric to see himself again in the way that I, and so many other people, saw him—as this incredible performer and even better man. To realize that he was Ric Flair and still all the amazing things he ever was.

Helping him to that point was a constant process, and at the end of it we were the best of friends because of it. But I don't want to make it seem like I did this just for him. I benefited very much as well. I was learning through it all. Damn, I know there were times I picked something up from him that he had no clue he was even teaching.

He's been in the business for thirty years. Just by being around him, I learn something every day.

Earlier on, I told you that the reason I like to pair up my shoulders and triceps in one session is because they're both pushing muscles, so the triceps get a pump when doing shoulder work. Well, the exact opposite is true for chest and biceps.

16. TRAINING YOUR CHEST AND BICEPS

I work these two muscle groups together because the chest is a pushing muscle, while biceps are pulling muscles. This difference in motion allows each body part to stay completely fresh while you're working the other one. When it comes to these two muscles, I want one hundred percent of my energy focused on their individual exercises.

I'm extremely strict on technique for all chest exercises. Too many chest exercises put your body in a position where getting hurt—tearing a pectoral muscle, for example—can happen at any moment. It's not worth the risk of injury just to add more weight on the bar to pump up your ego so you can tell your friends you benched a ton of weight at the gym the other day. Who cares if you end up getting hurt because of it?

With each rep, I squeeze and contract the pecs, concentrating on executing perfect form with manageable weight. There's just no need to use poundages you can't handle. I can make 20 pounds feel heavy if I'm contracting my chest and pumping blood into the pec muscles with every rep.

Chest Exercise #1: Flat-Bench Barbell Press

The classic exercise, the good old "bench press." When done correctly, the bench press not only works your pecs, but it hits your triceps and front delts as well. This is just a great exercise for building overall size and strength to your chest.

Chest Exercise #2: Incline-Bench Barbell Press

You won't be able to lift as much weight with this exercise as you do with flat-back bench presses, but that's expected. This variation does a better job of isolating your upper pecs.

Chest Exercise #3: Flat-Bench Dumbbell Flye

Because you're bringing your arms across your chest with this exercise, rather than straight up and down like with a bench press, you're excluding your triceps here. This will make your pecs work even harder.

Chest Exercise #4: Standing Cable Crossover

An exercise that's able to target the inside of the pectoral muscle, an area that, when defined, gives your chest that real ripped look.

My forearms reap the
benefit of working the
E-Z Curl without straps
or other accessories.

Biceps Exercise #1: Barbell Curl

Use the E-Z Curl bar for this mass-building exercise because it's much easier on your wrists than a straight bar. Although I encourage the use of an E-Z bar here, you need to avoid using straps and other accessories on your exercises. Ignoring straps that help your grip on a barbell is just going to force your forearms to pick up the slack and get a great workout in the process.

Biceps Exercise #2: Concentration Curl

Concentration curls are the best arm exercise to add peak to the biceps. If you want to add some height on that arm when you flex in front of the ladies (or your mirror), make this exercise part of your routine. I do only 2 sets of these, at 10 and 12 reps.

Biceps Exercise #3: Preacher Curl

This exercise targets the lower part of the muscle, just adding an overall thickness to your arms. I do only 2 sets with these as well, looking to complete between 8 and 10 reps for each.

Biceps Exercise #4: Hammer Curl

In addition to adding size to the biceps, hammer curls also develop your forearms. When your forearms are pumped out, your entire arm has a solid look. You can substitute barbell wrist curls here if you prefer an exercise that takes the biceps out of the equation and isolates the forearm.

For detailed instructions on the exercises in this chapter, see color pages 28–43.

TRIPLE H

Not only did the McMahon-Helmsley Era change my professional life by firmly establishing me as the top heel in the industry, it also changed my personal life. Stephanie McMahon and I didn't really know each other that well before we did the story line. I mean, we

17. LIFE WITH STEPH

obviously knew each other from work, but we didn't know each other personally at all. She hadn't spent much time around me and I hadn't spent much time around her.

Once we started working together on the show, we were around each other a lot, just doing "work stuff" at first. I think when you meet the person you're going to fall in love with, there is a connection right away to a certain degree. That connection was there for us, but neither of us recognized it. Other people did. Other people would make comments. I know Vince mentioned something to Steph about it long before the thought entered either of our minds. When it did finally hit the two of us, it was difficult. This wasn't just some regular romance. It's not like I took a look at her one day and thought, *Oh wow, she's cute. I think I'll ask her out on a date.* No way. I was committing career suicide getting involved in this. I had strong feelings for this person, but who knew how it would turn out. If it didn't work out in any way, I'm out of work. I'm out of the only thing I know how to do in life.

I knew it was a huge risk to take. Wrestling is the passion of my life. It's not just a nine-to-five job for me, and it's not like I could've just picked up and gone somewhere else to do it if things with Steph didn't work out. This is it. You're either working at WWE or you're not working.

And it was no easier for Steph. Her getting involved with a wrestler just wasn't something she was allowed to do. Her father and mother certainly never encouraged her to get romantically involved with one of the boys. It was something they had always tried to steer her away from.

With all this to consider, it took us a long time to get together. We each real-ized we had feelings for each other, but also knew that we couldn't just ignore this large obstacle in our way. So the relationship slowly built over time. We were spending more time around each other due to work, but then we'd find ourselves hanging around each other at TV when we didn't necessarily need to be. One day we started talking on the phone. I'd find a business reason to call her and then we'd stay talking for hours and hours about everything else. We were like two school kids with a crush. But due to the situation we were in, this was how it had to be.

There came a point when we both realized the feelings weren't dying down and we finally got together. Before anything happened romantically, we spoke to Vince about the situation and he told us it was okay with him. Soon after that, though, he changed his mind. He said he gave it more thought and realized, "This won't work out. You two cannot do this." He took it away just like that.

From Vince's standpoint, I can understand why he did this. I don't think he was screwing with us, he was confused about the situation as well. He had to make a decision as both a father and a businessman. As an emotional dad he's thinking, *I want my daughter to be happy, but if this doesn't work out it could alter my daughter's reputation with everyone in the business. Is it worth it?* The professional businessman has to think, *Is this good for business? Hunter is one of my top talents, what if it doesn't work out and he hurts my daughter? It's a total fiasco.*

How do you deal with that? I don't know and neither did he at first. To add to Vince's confusion about the situation, opinions came from every direction. Other wrestlers, agents, everybody shared their thoughts on what should happen between Steph and me.

There's a lot of politics in our business. Vince hates that word "politics," but that's what it is. During my early days on the independent scene, I was told, "There's a gun to your head every day in this business. It's up to you not to put the bullets in." Meaning: don't give anybody any ammo to kill your career with.

Screw the gun; I handed over the atomic bomb with this. If you don't think there was a line of people waiting to set it off and blow up my career, you're insane.

When we were forced apart, a lot of people thought they had squashed it and it was over. Although, one of the things going on that pissed them off was that they were expecting my relationship with Vince to deteriorate during this time too—and it didn't. It actually became more of a personal relationship, so it was moving in the opposite way people were expecting.

As for Steph and me, we tried to adhere to Vince's wishes and cool it off, but after a while it just didn't work. It was too late to stop. We were in love. We ended up getting back together after about ten months, and Vince gave us the green light for good this time.

Once we got back together, people really started to get negative about my role in the company and how it was bullshit that I was still working but also helping make decisions. It bothered me somewhat at first because I felt that so many of the same people who two years earlier were praising me—

We split up to avoid backstage politics, but Stephanie and I just couldn't fight it; we were in love.

"You're the hardest-working guy in the business," they'd say, or "The shit you're doing right now is the greatest thing in the entire industry"—were now saying I had no talent, no ability, and the only reason I was in the top spot at all was because I was "banging the boss's daughter."

This kind of bullshit pissed me off, but it never ruined my life or anything like that. I got over it quickly. For one thing, I knew that I had reached the top long before I ever knew Stephanie. Something else that helped me incredibly over this time was my experience with Shawn back in the day. He had faced a similar situation.

Before he became the World Champion, Shawn was perceived as the greatest wrestler ever. People treated him like the Second Coming. The instant they put the title on him, those same people turned on him. "Shawn Michaels sucks! He's a namby-pamby champion. He's a sissy." It was unbelievable how hard they turned on him.

And it bothered Shawn. It ate Shawn alive. He couldn't deal with these pathetic, jealous nobodies and eventually, I believe, that was a big part of what started Shawn down the road of personal problems that plagued him over the years.

When he became the champion, business wasn't stellar, so people said it was all his fault, that he could never carry the company. None of that was fair. They were all lies rooted in envy. In truth, not only was Shawn a great champion for that time, he is one of the greatest of all time.

Having been through all this with Shawn, I knew how meaningless all the petty bullshit was and it helped me deal with what people were throwing at me because of my relationship with Steph. I realized none of it was worth the energy I'd have to spend thinking about it. They're just opinions and they don't matter. As long as I know that I only do what's right for the business—regardless of how something affects my character—as long as that remains true, I'll be okay.

There are still some guys in our business who hate me over this or who think I'm a horrible person. That's fine, that's their opinion. I know that for every one of those people, there's at least one guy that I've helped or I get along with great that I've worked with and if you ask any of those guys if I'm this selfish, pompous prick, they would tell you, "You're nuts." And if you still don't believe it, and you still think I'm this big jerk, well then, you can just kiss my ass because I don't know what else I can say about it.

A lot of the people who were after me have given up, though. They see that not only are Stephanie and I married, but the love we share is so strong, so real, they don't have a chance to destroy it.

To me, one of the wonderful things about Steph and our relationship is that the two of us don't only have each other, we also have two families who we are incredibly close to. My mom and dad, Paul and Pat Levesque, are the best parents on earth. And my sister, Lynn, brother-in-law, Gordon, and niece and nephew—Neysa and Pete—are just such wonderful people. I'm blessed to have them all in my life. The fact that Steph is as close to her family as I am to mine is one of the things that pulled us together at first. We both have a respect for family and a deep appreciation of where we came from.

And now we have become a part of each other's family. I don't even think of them as *her* family or a secondary family; they are *my* family. I hope Steph feels that way about my side as well. I know my parents consider her their daughter. When I say this, I realize how lucky we are to have these relationships in our lives.

Sometimes I think—and this is going to sound corny as hell—but how can one person get to have all of these things?

Steph and I are fortunate to have each other and enjoy career success. And I'm not just talking financially, I'm also talking creatively. We are both doing the one thing we love in this world. At the end of the day, we feel fulfilled by our jobs. Then we have these amazing families who love us dearly. I'm aware that not everybody gets to have all of this, and I do truly consider myself fortunate.

But don't think for a second that having all of this is going to make me coast from here on out. Just like when you're in the weight room, in life, complacency sucks. You can never be one hundred percent satisfied with where you are. You have to keep setting goals, keep striving to reach the next level.

Remember when I was sitting down in Alabama, thinking about what it meant to have a career-ending injury and all that kept running through my mind was, *I'm not done yet! There's still so much I want to accomplish.* Well, that still holds true today. The Game is nowhere near over. There are still so many things I need to do. Goals I need to reach. Milestones I need to surpass.

In the ring and in life. And nothing—or no one—is going to prevent me from achieving them all.

Do not let anything stop you from reaching your dreams. Visualize what you want to achieve. Set goals. Stop making excuses. Motivate yourself to accomplish anything you can imagine.

Now get out there and do it.

As a little boy I had a dream, and my parents gave me all the support and more that I needed to follow that dream. And for that I cannot thank them enough. They allowed me to be anything I wanted to be, and they have always been my biggest fans. My parents were always there for me and taught me the importance of family. My entire family had a hand in where I am today.

ACKNOWLEDGMENTS

My sister, Lynn, and her husband, Gordon, with their two children, Pete and Neysa, prove to me every day that they have always been behind me and my dream. My extended family, the McMahons—Vince and Linda: thank you for building a domain that has offered me an opportunity to live a life I could never have dreamed of and for making the best thing in my life, Steph. Success doesn't mean much without someone to share it with, and I found the perfect person. Steph, you are my heart and soul. I love you.

For the "boys": Walter "Killer" Kowalski, thank you for breaking me in the right way, the "old school" way.

Terry Taylor, you helped me polish a rough stone and are a true friend. To Terry's family, my "Atlanta family," thank you for taking me in. "The Nature Boy" Ric Flair, you have always been an inspiration to me and you're now a great friend. To the "Clique"—Kevin Nash, Shawn Michaels, Sean Waltman, and Scott Hall—Mark Callaway, Steven Regal, Pat Patterson, Jack Lanza, Jerry Brisco, Arn Anderson, Kevin Dunn, J.R., and The King, you are the best at what you do; thank you. To every Superstar to lace up the boots before me, thank you for paving the way.

Brian Zagorites, I want to thank you for being a friend and a mentor, and for molding me like a big brother should. Charles Glass, Mike Watson, and N3, you are the best at what you do. For those "behind" the scenes: Barry Bloom and company, for their tireless work; thank you just doesn't seem enough. Ann Gordon, for always helping me get where I'm going in more ways than one. Lucas, for your patience in writing the book with me. Stacey Pascarella helped me make this book a reality. And to everyone at WWE from top to bottom: you are a link in the chain of the company's success.

To the Seattle Seahawks and Kent Johnson, a special thanks for loaning us the use of the training facility. Also thank you to anyone else I may have forgotten—that doesn't mean you are not important, it's just that I am writing this after traveling ten hours to Helsinki, Finland, then going out all night with the Nature Boy, wrestling a sold-out show, and now taking a bumpy bus ride back to the hotel—oh yeah, and the deadline was yesterday. (Sorry, Stacey.) Still, thank you to everyone!

Again, for the little boy who had a dream and the people who allowed that dream to become a reality.